Praise for *Render unto Caesar*

"It would be an understatement to call *Render unto Caesar* thought-provoking. Though it is a small book, nearly every page challenges readers to step out of their religious comfort zone."

—ANN CARNAHAN, *Rocky Mountain News*

"A thorough and timely analysis of political morality and its relation to [Catholic] teaching . . . Archbishop Chaput works patiently and with keen intelligence through the false myths and fake rights that control our political life."

—CARDINAL FRANCIS GEORGE, O.M.I., archbishop of Chicago

"[Chaput] has written a book that is informed, measured, civil, and pointed. It should be read, discussed, taken to heart in the United States and beyond."

—REVEREND ROBERT IMBELLI, *L'Osservatore Romano*

"[Chaput] gives his readers a magnificent vision of what precisely living as a faithful Catholic entails, reminding Catholics, clerical *and* lay, that they are called to holiness, to be saints, to love with a redemptive love, to sanctify their work, and to change the world, including the political world in which they live, for the better."

—WILLIAM E. MAY, *FCS Quarterly*

"[Chaput's] prose is unfailingly calm and considerate, yet reveals a keen sense of irony and a formidable wit."

—MICHAEL J. MILLER, *The Catholic World Report*

"For Catholics who've grown weary of hearing leaders and would-be leaders spout platitudes in place of hard truths, [Chaput] comes as a breath of fresh air. The archbishop of Denver tells it like it is."

—RUSSELL SHAW, *Our Sunday Visitor*

"Chaput moves decisively against the prevailing cultural tide in the media, in the universities, among political activists; a tide that wants to thrust the faith from the public stage."

—SANDRO MAGISTER, chiesa.espressonline.it

"Succinct and shrewd, and better than those [books on faith and politics] by most scholar specialists who make a living in these neighborhoods."

—GERALD V. BRADLEY, National Review Online

"A terrific book for all Catholics . . . A gratifyingly concise, lucid lesson about Catholicism in America: its history, past struggles, and current conundrums."

—MARIA MCFADDEN, *Human Life Review*/Catholic Eye

"[*Render Unto Caesar*] should be read by every Catholic and far beyond that flock as well. Any person of faith interested in the growing pressure to banish faith from the public square or troubled by [the] new atheism will be encouraged by Chaput's bold and clear defense of Christian participation in the debates of the day as Christians. Order one for yourself, and send one to an agnostic/atheist friend."

—HUGH HEWITT, Townhall.com

RENDER UNTO CAESAR

RENDER UNTO CAESAR

SERVING THE NATION BY LIVING
OUR CATHOLIC BELIEFS
IN POLITICAL LIFE

CHARLES J. CHAPUT, O.F.M. Cap.

IMAGE BOOKS
DOUBLEDAY

NEW YORK   LONDON
TORONTO   SYDNEY   AUCKLAND

Published in the United States by Image, an imprint of the Crown
Publishing Group, a division of Random House LLC,
a Penguin Random House Company, New York.
www.crownpublishing.com

IMAGE is a registered trademark, and the "I" colophon
is a trademark of Random House LLC.

Originally published in hardcover in slightly different form in
the United States by Doubleday Religion, a division of Random
House LLC, a Penguin Random House Company, New York,
in 2008, and subsequently in paperback by
Image Books, an imprint of the Crown Publishing Group,
a division of Random House LLC,
a Penguin Random House Company, New York, in 2009.

A Cataloging-in-Publication record has been established for
*Render Unto Caesar: Serving the Nation by Living our Catholic Beliefs in
Political Life* under the ISBN 978-0-385-52229-8

ISBN 978-0-385-36446-1

Printed in the United States of America

Book design by Ellen Cipriano
Cover photograph of Augustus Denarius coin: © Joe Geranio

1   2   3   4   5   6   7   8   9   10

First Proprietary Edition

IN MEMORY OF JAMES T. McHUGH,
bishop and friend

Freedom is a system based on courage.

—*Péguy*

The motive power of democracy is love.

—*Bergson*

CONTENTS

RENDER UNTO CAESAR

1.

STARTING AT THE SOURCE

I WROTE THIS BOOK for two reasons. The first is simple. A friend asked me to do it.

My friend is a young attorney. In 2004, he ran for the Colorado General Assembly on the Democratic Party ticket. He did surprisingly well. He lost by a small margin in a heavily Republican district. But it was an odd experience. He was barely thirty and new to campaigning. His older opponent had an advantage as the incumbent. Worse, he was a political "blue," but running in traditionally red territory.

Even his own party saw him as a strange creature. My friend believed then and believes now that *Roe v. Wade* is bad law. Thus, he had trouble with some of his own Democratic colleagues from the day he chose to run. He found out how hard it is to raise money. He felt the same heavy pressure all candidates feel to adjust their principles to win support. What he discovered—like many others—is that being a faithful Catholic in political life is often easier said than done. Some months after the election, he asked me to write down my thoughts about Catholics in public service to help people considering a political career. I agreed.

The irony, though, is this: A very good guide to Catholic citizenship and public leadership already exists. The pastoral statement *Living the Gospel of Life,* issued in 1998 by the U.S. Catholic bishops—though it had to survive a great deal of internal friction and wrangling first—remains, in my view, the best tool anywhere for understanding the American Catholic political vocation.[1] Catholics already know that politics exists to serve the common good. But what is the common good? It's a thorny question. Some problems are more complicated than others. Some issues have more gravity than others. Some methods to achieve a good end are wrong in themselves. We can never choose them without coarsening the society we inhabit.

Public officials have a special responsibility in sorting these things out. This is why the health of our public life requires men and women of strong moral character in political service. No community understands this better than the Catholic Church, from centuries of both good and ugly experience. The genius of Pope John Paul II's great 1995 encyclical, *Evangelium Vitae* (The Gospel of Life), is not that it gives us a specific, sectarian blueprint for building a moral society. It doesn't. Rather, it offers a common architecture for humane political thought and boundaries for government action that cannot be crossed without brutalizing human dignity. When the U.S. bishops issued *Living the Gospel of Life,* they applied the best of John Paul's encyclical to the American experience. Not surprisingly, no other document ever issued by the American bishops on political responsibility has the clarity, coherence, and force of *Living the Gospel of Life.* The only sadness is that so few Catholics seem to know about it. In fact, if this book does nothing more than lead more people to read and act on *Living the Gospel of Life,* it will have partly served its purpose.

The second reason for this book is more personal. Like many other pastors, I deal with the human problems that drive public policy every day: homelessness, poverty, abortion, immigration, and a dozen other issues. No one addresses these problems more directly or effectively than the Catholic Church and other religious communities. Over the past decade I've grown increasingly tired of the church and her people being told to be quiet on public issues that urgently concern us. Worse, Catholics themselves too often stay silent out of a misguided sense of good manners. Even those of us who are bishops can sometimes seem more concerned with discretion and diplomacy than speaking plainly and acting clearly. Do not misunderstand me. Discretion and diplomacy are essential skills—but not if they lead to a habit of self-censorship. Self-censorship is an even bigger mistake than allowing ourselves to be lectured by people with little sympathy for our beliefs.

Let me explain what this book will *not* do. It will not endorse any political party or candidate. Both major U.S. political parties have plenty of good people in their ranks. Neither party fully represents a Catholic way of thinking about social issues. One of the lessons we need to learn from the last fifty years is that a preferred American "Catholic" party doesn't exist. The sooner Catholics feel at home in *any* political party, the sooner that party begins to take them for granted and then to ignore their concerns. Party loyalty is a dead end. It's a lethal form of laziness. Issues matter. Character matters. Acting on principle matters. The sound bite and the slogan do not matter. They belong to a vocabulary of the herd, and human beings deserve better. Real freedom demands an ability to think, and a great deal of modern life seems deliberately designed to discourage that.

This book will not feed anyone's nostalgia for a Catholic golden age. The past usually looks better as it fades in the rearview mirror. Art Buchwald once said that if you like nostalgia, pretend today is yesterday and then go out and have a great time. I agree. After listening to some ten thousand personal confessions over thirty-seven years of priesthood, I'm very confident that the details of daily life change over time, but human nature doesn't. We've seen better and worse times to be Catholic in the

United States than the present. But today is the time in which we need to work.

This book will not be an academic study or a work of formal scholarship. I've included endnotes where I believe them to be useful or necessary, but they are not exhaustive. On the other hand, this book certainly *does* claim to be a statement of common sense amply supported by history, public record, and fact. Readers will also notice that I reference Joseph Ratzinger in various ways throughout this book, but not because of his election in 2005 as Pope Benedict XVI. At least, this is not the main reason. In fact, popes serve, contribute, fade like everyone else and recede into the memory of the church. People usually assume that popes, and all pastors, have far more "power" over events than they actually do.

As successor of Peter, Joseph Ratzinger is a pastor for all Catholics, including American Catholics. But equally important, the course of his life and the development of his thought—as an author, intellectual, and teacher; from his time as a seminarian in the Third Reich, to young theologian, to bishop, to cardinal, to confidant and close adviser to John Paul II, to his own election as pope—offer a unique window on the course of Catholic life in the twentieth and early twenty-first centuries. He belongs to an extraordinary generation of Catholic leaders who lived through war and genocide, remained faithful to Jesus Christ, never lost their love for the church, and struggled hard to renew her mission to the world; a generation we should learn from and which, when it passes, will not come again.

Finally, this book doesn't offer any grand theory. It does offer thoughts based on my nineteen years as an American Catholic bishop and my interest in our common history. I believe that our nation's public life, like Christianity itself, is meant for everyone, and everyone has a duty to contribute to it. The American experiment depends on the active involvement of all its citizens, not just lobbyists, experts, think tanks, and the mass media. For Catholics, politics—the pursuit of justice and the common good—is part of the history of salvation. No one is a minor actor in that drama. Each person is important.

I grew up in Concordia, Kansas. It's a typical small farming community of fewer than seven thousand people. But in those days—the 1950s—Concordia was also the hometown of Senator Frank Carlson, who played a major role in Congress. So it wasn't unusual for people in Concordia to think they had something valuable to say about politics and life in Washington, D.C. That's the way it should be. That's what the founders and framers of our country intended. Every reasonably intelligent person—which means just about all of us—has something important to add to the discussion of our nation's future. In this book, I speak as a Catholic citizen to fellow American Catholics and other interested Christians. But I hope many other people of good heart will see the importance of these issues and find value in these pages. Ultimately, I believe that all of us who call ourselves American and Catholic need to recover what it really means to be "Catholic." We also need to find again the courage to be *Catholic Christians first*—not in opposition to our country, but to serve its best ideals.

ARCHBISHOP JOHN IRELAND, who liked a good fight, said many decades ago that "if great things are not done by Catholics in America, the fault lies surely with themselves—not with the republic."[2] I sometimes wonder how Ireland might have answered Ted Turner's famous crack that Christianity is a religion for losers.[3] It would be a debate worth paying to see.

Ireland served as a chaplain in the Civil War. He was a forceful, opinionated, energetic man; more than a match for any Turner-style media czar. He was an early supporter of racial equality. Presidents William McKinley and Theodore Roosevelt called him a friend. And he was a strong booster of the American experiment—in fact, too strong a booster, which caused him friction with the Holy See and many of his brother bishops. If he were alive today, I suspect Ireland would still be bullish on America. But he might be baffled by our nation's weirdly divided heart about religion over the last fifty years. The crude anti-Catholic bigotry of the nineteenth and early twentieth centuries—the kind so familiar to Archbishop

Ireland—has mutated into something different. In our age, it involves an elitist contempt for religion in general, but Christianity in particular.

The late historian Christopher Lasch saw that today, "it is [the leadership classes]—those who control the international flow of money and information, preside over philanthropic foundations and institutions of higher learning, manage the instruments of cultural production and thus set the terms of public debate—that have lost faith in the values" of the American experiment and Western culture in general. In their self-reliance and overconfidence, our "thinking classes have seceded not just from the common world around them but from reality itself."[4]

I remember those words from Lasch every time someone warns me that Catholics shouldn't try to "impose their beliefs" on society. I recall his words whenever I read yet another unhappy opinion columnist urging Christians to respect—*revere* is often closer to the intended meaning—the separation of church and state.

In fact, Catholics strongly support a proper and healthy separation of the civil and religious dimensions in our national life. History is a great teacher, and one of its lessons is that when religion and the state mingle too intimately, bad things can happen to both. But of course, everything depends on what people mean by a *proper* and *healthy* separation. Some persons do sincerely and deeply worry about religion hijacking public life. I respect their views. I also find their worries excessive. I agree that religious people who act or speak rashly can cause such fears. But too often, I find that both of these slogans—"don't impose your beliefs on society" and "the separation of church and state"—have little to do with fact. Instead, they're used as debating tools; a kind of verbal voodoo. People employ them to shut down serious thought, like the *four legs good, two legs bad* chorus in Orwell's novel *Animal Farm*. George Orwell had little love for the Catholic Church. But he had even less for the debasement of facts through pious-sounding political slogans. The truth is, *no one* in mainstream American politics wants a theocracy. *No one* in mainstream public life wants to force uniquely Catholic doctrines into federal law. So we need to see these slogans for what they frequently are: foolish and sometimes dishonest arguments that confuse our national memory and identity.

The "God question" is part of our public life, and we simply can't avoid it. *Does God exist or not?* Each citizen answers that in his or her own way. But the issue is not theoretical. It goes to first premises. It has very practical implications, just as it did at our country's founding. If we *really* believe God exists, that belief will inevitably color our personal and public behavior: our actions, our choices, and our decisions. It will also subtly frame our civic language and institutions. If we really believe God exists, excluding God from our public life—whether we do it explicitly through Supreme Court action or implicitly by our silence as citizens—cannot serve the common good because it amounts to enshrining the unreal in the place of the real.

People who take God seriously will not remain silent about their faith. They will often disagree about doctrine or policy, but they won't be quiet. They can't be. They'll act on what they believe, sometimes at the cost of their reputations and careers. Obviously the common good demands a respect for other people with different beliefs and a willingness to compromise whenever possible. But for Catholics, the common good can never mean muting themselves in public debate on foundational issues of faith or human dignity. Christian faith is always personal but never private. This is why any notion of tolerance that tries to reduce faith to a private idiosyncrasy, or a set of opinions that we can indulge at home but need to be quiet about in public, will always fail. As a friend once said, it's like asking a married man to act single in public. He can certainly do that—but he won't stay married for long.

THE ACTOR JAMES PUREFOY once played the early Roman leader Mark Antony. He told an interviewer that he had been stunned, in studying for his role, by the routine brutality of pre-Christian Rome.[5] Very few moderns can grasp what ancient society was like, he said, because "even if you are agnostic, even if you're an atheist," Christian morals profoundly frame the way you think and live. The Christian system of values is "written all the way through all our actions, all the time." Christianity has so deeply shaped our environment that we take it for granted. Even people who have no faith at all live in a world largely created by the Christian faith.

I mention this because it connects in an odd way with an experience a friend of mine related while I was working on this book. On April 7, 2007, she returned a book to a local library. It was a Saturday. On the library door she saw a little sign that said, Closed Sunday. That struck her as strange. The libraries in her metro area are always open on Sunday. She drove to another library. She found the same sign. In the end, she visited seven different libraries in three different library districts. All of them typically open their doors on Sunday. All of them had similar Closed Sunday signs, but no explanation.

Of course April 8, 2007, was Easter Sunday. Easter is an inescapably *Christian* feast. It can't be fully secularized, no matter how many chocolate bunnies and painted eggs pile up around it. The Resurrection, coming on the heels of a very unpleasant execution, is not an easily tamed story. And *exactly this story*—the fact of Jesus Christ's crucifixion and resurrection from the dead—is the starting point, the source, the *seed* that became the faith, the moral code, the sense of human dignity, the culture, and the civilization we now take for granted every day.

Classical thought, Judaism, and the Enlightenment

also played important roles in forming the American mind. But Christians, in a uniquely powerful way, did the building of the American nation. At its best, that nation is an open and humane one, with plenty of room for other-believers and nonbelievers. But if we repudiate the source of our identity—if we treat the religious dimension of our shared public life as a word we don't mention in explaining a civic holiday—we're headed for real confusion.

Maybe the libraries my friend visited were afraid of Americans United for the Separation of Church and State. Maybe thousands of other libraries across the country *do,* in fact, celebrate Easter; but if they do, there's nothing theocratic about it, and the founders would fully understand.

Like it or not, American Catholics are part of a struggle over our country's identity and future. If this book helps some of us rediscover what it really means to be Catholic—the purpose of our time in the world, the lessons of our history, the responsibilities of citizenship, and the implications of the Christian faith we claim to believe—then it succeeds. We have obligations as believers. We have duties as citizens. We need to honor both, or we honor neither.

2.

MEN WITHOUT CHESTS

WE'VE ALWAYS ENVIED EUROPE. We don't like to admit it. But even today, in politics, economics, and religion, the American pedigree sooner or later tracks back to Europe. Secretly Americans worry that when it comes to art, food, architecture, music, culture—well, we just don't measure up. And Europeans are often glad to agree. In fact, Europe has taught Americans a great many things. Many of those lessons have been profoundly valuable. But unfortunately, one of the latest lessons is this: A public life that excludes God does not enrich the human spirit. It kills it.

During the 2007 French presidential race won by Nicolas Sarkozy, the bishop of Lyon, Cardinal Philippe Barbarin, urged Christians to "speak out more . . . defending what, in the view of Christians, is right for everyone." He warned that democracy is only a means for pursuing justice; it isn't God, it isn't an end in itself, and it can sometimes lose its moral compass. He also pressed

Christian political leaders to model their faith more visibly through their public service.[1]

To our ears, his words may sound mild. But France is not the United States. It has a very different history. Lyon's first bishop, Pothinus, died in prison in AD 177 before the Roman authorities could publicly execute him. Many of his fellow local Christians died by mob violence or in the arena. Still, the Christian faith grew rapidly. It produced great saints and suffered equally great sinners. In fact, it touched nearly all of French life until the coming of the Enlightenment and Revolution, which attacked Christianity in the name of human reason.

French history is thus both deeply Catholic and deeply anticlerical. The nation that Catholics still call the "eldest daughter of the church" also gave birth to the Committee of Public Safety and the Terror. It nurtured Thérèse of Lisieux and Voltaire, Jacques Maritain and Jean-Jacques Rousseau. In recent years, a belligerently secular France led the way in purging any reference to Europe's Christian past from a proposed European constitution.

France has a divided soul in a way few Americans can understand. When Cardinal Barbarin spoke to his countrymen in 2007, six of the ten leading presidential candidates described themselves as atheists. In a country with nineteen centuries of Christian memory, with a cultural legacy profoundly marked by Christian faith, and with a nominally Catholic majority, fewer than one in eight people now attend Mass on a weekly basis.[2] The church is dwindling. And so are the French themselves. Despite government incentives, the native French birthrate lags below replacement levels.[3] Crime has increased, along with racial hatred, economic grievances, and immigrant violence.[4] The nation's most dynamic new presence is Islam. One-third of all Muslims in Europe now live in France, and a steady stream of vigorous Islamic propaganda pours into the country from the Middle East.[5] The country's primatial Catholic See—Lyon, the ancient See of Saint Irenaeus, one of the early doctors of the church—is now also the home of the Islamist Tawhid Center.

What we believe about God shapes what we believe about men and women. And what we believe about men and women shapes how we act—socially, politically, and economically. The Christian belief in God differs from Islamic belief in serious ways. So do Christian and Islamic ideas about the nature of the human person. These differences have far-reaching practical consequences, including *political* consequences. But rapid Muslim growth isn't the only reason for the identity crisis now gripping secular France and much of Europe. The continent's real problem lies deeper. Islam is merely filling a hole in the chest of an ailing civilization. Europe has an illness of its own choosing: a hollowing out of its spirit through pride, greed, self-absorption, the rejection of children, the exclusion of God, and contempt for its own past, including its Christian soul.

Before his election as Pope Benedict XVI, Joseph Ratzinger warned that "Europe has developed a culture that, in a manner hitherto unknown to mankind, excludes God from public awareness." He said an inner emptiness now cripples Europe "that is the most radical contradiction not only of Christianity but of all the religious and moral traditions of humanity."[6] Europe's demographic decline—the sharpest in seven centuries, not counting new immigrants from outside the continent—is merely the outer sign of an inner hollowness.[7]

Of course, France is not the United States. Europe is not the United States. In some ways we're very different. But we do share a civilization. The ties that relate us make it easier for a problem in one house to migrate to the other. We create the future by our choices and our actions, here and now. That includes our choices in the public square. Cardinal Barbarin merely said the obvious when he urged French Catholics to engage their nation's political life more vigorously, guided by their Catholic faith. The hour for his message was late, and the audience was small; but at least he spoke the truth. American Catholics might do well to listen and learn. We need to examine our own nation's experiences accordingly.

• • •

TIP O'NEILL, FORMER Speaker of the U.S. House of Representatives, once said, "All politics is local." He was talking about how local facts shape Washington politics. Public policy, no matter how well designed, stands or falls on how it touches the local citizen, including the "citizens" of a family. A friend of mine once described listening to an argument against rent-controlled housing that sounded quite reasonable. Rent control, the logic went, discourages new housing projects because builders can't make enough profit from their investment. Therefore, rent control hurts the poor and middle-class families who most need the lower rents that come from a bigger supply of rental housing units. Unfortunately, my friend lived in a rent-controlled apartment with his three children and his wife, who handled the family money. She thought rent control made a lot of sense—and therefore, so did he.

All politics is local, and so is every other important aspect of life. All that federal money for medical research can seem unreal and remote until someone you love—your spouse or friend or child—depends on a cure. Then it seems good. Then it seems urgent.

One of the achievements of American life is that the average local citizen has experienced this country as so good and so representative of his or her beliefs for so long. Yet America has always been more than a patchwork of people pursuing enlightened self-interest. We're not just a strong economic machine. Rather, we *have* a strong economic machine because *something else,* something deeper, has always powered it. America runs on an ideal of the human person. More precisely, it draws its life from a belief in each person's innate dignity and potential for greatness. A set of founding principles weaves local citizens into one people and one country. Thus, the United States has always been a nation of individuals bound together in a common cause of opportunity and freedom. The world has many other democracies. Many work. Some work very well. But none has worked so well, for so long, for so many people.

Our success surrounds us. We take it for granted. Yet American life contrasts sharply with much of the rest of the world—especially those regions where most of humanity actually lives. The average life span in South Africa is fifty-one. In India, it's sixty-two. But American men can expect to live to nearly seventy-eight and women to eighty.[8] That's double the life span of Americans in the mid-nineteenth century. More than 70 percent of American young people graduate from high school.[9] About one in three attend high school in Latin America, but many fail to graduate.[10] Sub-Saharan Africa is even worse. Only 12 percent of young people finish a secondary education.[11] Meanwhile the average per capita U.S. personal income, already among the highest in the world, nearly doubled between 1990 and 2005.[12] Grave poverty does exist in the United States, and it offers an ugly witness against the comfort and self-absorption now driving so much of American life. But it's nonetheless true that even the poor among U.S. citizens compare well with much of the rest of the world today.

Americans have huge advantages in their personal liberties, mobility, and consumer choices. The same applies for medicine, science, and technology. The United States is a nation based on law. Americans also take their laws seriously in a world where civil rights often exist only on paper. Among developed countries, the United States is the only one that officially promotes freedom of belief around the world through its U.S. Commission on International Religious Freedom.

As the author and *Washington Post* columnist Robert Samuelson wrote as early as 1995, "America today is a far wealthier and more compassionate society than 50 years ago, and on a personal level, most Americans appreciate these achievements."[13] But Samuelson, among others, noted even then that success had made Americans neither whole nor happy. Today, every step forward seems to drag along a revenge of unintended consequences. Technology has made U.S. workers more competitive. It has also deepened worker stress by overloading employees with information. It has also led to longer workdays and heavier demands for productivity. As a result, the United States now loses 200 million working days annually to work-related mental health problems. We spend up to $44 billion each year treating depression.[14] And depression now sets in at younger ages. About 2 percent of all school-age American children and up to 8 percent of all adolescents suffer from depression.[15]

While a consumer economy makes life easier, it also turns appetites into needs. Nobody makes us pile up credit card debt, but millions of Americans do exactly that. By 2005, Federal Reserve data showed that Americans had a "household debt to personal disposable income" ratio of 118 percent—in other words, they *owed* $1.18 for every dollar of their disposable income.[16] And though most Americans claim to revere the family, family life has clearly suffered in recent decades. Married couples are steadily declining as a percentage of U.S. households. Since 2000, unmarried opposite-sex couples have grown roughly 14 percent. In the same time frame, female couples grew 12 percent. Male couples grew 24 percent.[17] This has big implications for the American economy. It also shapes how children experience their families and early lives.

American students perform poorly in history, geography, and other key disciplines.[18] In 2003, only three major colleges in the United States required students to take a course on the U.S. Constitution to graduate—the three armed services academies.[19] Only 11 percent of U.S. high school seniors test as proficient in their own national history.[20] Some 29 percent of young American adults can't find the Pacific Ocean on a map.[21] In 2006, three years after the American-led invasion of Iraq, only

37 percent could locate the country where U.S. troops were fighting and dying.[22]

Maybe these are random facts. Maybe they suggest very little. As Benjamin Disraeli once said, "There are three kinds of lies: lies, damned lies and statistics." Numbers are a kind of magic. People can use them to prove just about anything. None of the current trends has a simple cause. American life has always been a mixture of ignorance and genius, piety and violence. But *something* in American life really has changed. We've become more vulgar and more callous. The 1999 Columbine massacre was new. The 2007 Virginia Tech massacre was new. The hate behind these and other killings in American schools showed a peculiar contempt not just for young human life but also for the project of learning that helps to ennoble it.

Over the past few decades, our civic vocabulary has coarsened. An overfed understanding of our personal rights and individual freedom has squeezed out the responsibility and decorum we owe to each other. Too many of us have become what the media scholar Neil Postman called Visigoths—people who value mob fashion over excellence in thought and taste—instead of Athenians.[23] The virus has different names. Robert Samuelson called it a spirit of entitlement that leads us "to believe that certain things are (or ought to be) guaranteed to us," like high-quality health care, global dominance, and personal fulfillment.[24] The scholar James Twitchell described it as a loss of common decency and a sense of shame.[25] Stanford University's William Damon called it a culture of indulgence.[26] And the sociologist Charles Derber named it as a "wilding" of America—in effect, a barbarization that comes from our greed and violence as we "pursue divisive and increasingly unattainable goals which cannot meet our deepest needs for respect, love and justice."[27]

Whatever we choose to call the present moment, some things seem plain. We have oceans of information, but personal isolation has grown. So has cynicism toward public life and service. So has an ugly spirit of irony that, in the words of Jedediah Purdy, "tends to discourage civic involvement of all sorts. From local school boards to congressional campaigns, politics means taking public stands, throwing in one's lot with a standard bearer, and constantly risking being caught out as a hypocrite, a sucker or a naïve minority of one."[28] In other words, for too many of us, it seems safer to be a smug coward than somebody with a spine who might lose.

Over the past five decades, the United States has ranked lowest among the world's established democracies in voter turnout.[29] And Americans' grip on their own government has also slipped. Nothing says it better than a roster of Washington lobbyists—about thirty-five thousand, or sixty-four for every member of Congress. The number of lobbyists doubled between 2000 and

2005. And client fees grew as much as 100 percent. In the words of one political scientist, "the growth of lobbying makes . . . the balance between those with resources and those without resources" even worse than it already was.[30]

Whatever the signs of the times teach us, it can't be complacency.

IN THE PAST, faced with deep social divisions, Americans have usually turned to God. In our roots, we're a religious people. All of the religious Great Awakenings in our history have followed periods of great national anxiety, like the struggle over slavery. But today, some people see God himself as the problem—and with him, the believers who claim to follow him. The name of the God problem is "religious extremism." And since Christianity has always been the main religious faith in the United States, the real target of today's elite antireligious resentment is usually the Christian believer. More precisely, it's many of those Christians who actually practice their faith; who rely on it to guide their actions in public as well as in private life.[31]

The modern phobia of God comes in two styles: hard and soft. The hard brand—the explicit atheism pushed by celebrity unbelievers like the writer Sam Harris, the scientist Richard Dawkins, and others—is more vocal; more *evangelical.* It's also more honest. Predictably, the panache of evangelical atheism appeals to the media. But in real impact, it may also be less important.

Hard, "scientific" atheism depends on an almost liturgical draping of unbelief with the vestments of science. But even among scientists themselves, a significant minority does claim to be religious.[32] Francis Collins, the head of the Human Genome Project, is explicitly Christian. John Polkinghorne, the respected particle physicist, is also an Anglican theologian. Science has great power as a tool. It's enormously valuable for exploring material reality. But presuming that all *real* reality is material is a form of *belief*—and for most people, a deeply unsatisfying one.

That doesn't stop Dawkins from comparing Abrahamic religions to loaded guns, or describing faith itself as "one of the world's great evils, comparable to the smallpox virus, but harder to eradicate."[33] But when he does, he's using his skills as a preacher, not as a biologist. As John Polkinghorne said more plainly, he's having an "atheistic rant."[34] And we can understand why. God was supposed to have the good manners to go away. But God didn't get the memo. In fact, religion seems as strong as ever. Data from the Pew Forum on Religion and Public Life show that the growth and public impact of religion have in some ways *increased* worldwide, especially in the global South.[35] To borrow a thought from the sociologist Peter Berger, the really strange thing about modern life is not the existence of intense religious commitment but those academics and intellectuals who find it odd.[36]

Among unbelievers, this persistence of religion can lead to awkwardly unscientific outbursts. Sam Harris, returning from a meeting at the Salk Institute, wrote, "While at Salk, I witnessed scientists giving voice to some of the most unctuous religious apologies I have ever heard. It is one thing to be told that the pope is a great champion of reason and that his opposition to embryonic stem cell research has nothing to do with religious dogmatism; it is quite another to be told this by a Stanford physician who sits on the President's Council on Bioethics." Harris complained that "there were several moments during our panel discussions [at Salk] that brought to mind the final scene of *Invasion of the Body Snatchers*—people who looked like scientists, had published as scientists, and would soon be returning to their labs, nevertheless gave voice to the alien hiss of religious lunacy at the slightest prodding."[37]

Contempt is usually a sign of weakness. What makes the hard brand of unbelief more offensive but probably also less dangerous is that it's so naked. The heart of celebrity atheism's claim is that atheists are smart, and believers are dumb. Therefore it's *just not fair* that anyone takes religious faith seriously.

Christians believe that God created all persons in his image. *Because* of that, and only because of that, all persons have inalienable rights. That includes unbelievers. From a Catholic point of view, people without religious faith are just as capable of superior intelligence, good-will, and natural virtue as anyone else. They do, and should, have the same freedom to express their convictions in the public square as any other citizen—including, of course, religious believers.

Scientific atheism's contempt for faith is, in its effect, the glue for a new kind of knowledge oligarchy. The bad news is that so many members of this new class seem to lean toward B. F. Skinner's call for abolishing the "spuriously honorific" sense of humanity "defended by the literatures of freedom and dignity." The Christian scholar C. S. Lewis once famously warned of the "abolition of man"—that is, the destruction of what makes human beings "human"—by a scientific and technological elite.[38] Skinner was well aware of Lewis's argument, and he specifically answered Lewis in *Beyond Freedom and Dignity* with the words: "To man *qua* man, we readily say good riddance. Only by dispossessing him can we turn to the real causes of human behavior. Only then can we turn from the inferred to the observed, from the miraculous to the natural, from the inaccessible to *the manipulable* [emphasis added]."[39]

This kind of knowledge-class bigotry amounts to barbarism with a graduate degree. As the great Protestant theologian Reinhold Niebuhr once said, "A barbarism developed in the heart of civilization has one

important advantage over genuinely primitive bar-
barisms. It avails itself of all the technical advantages of
civilization."[40]

The softer brand of God-aversion takes a different
approach. It rewrites history, subtly uses fear, and appeals
to American generosity to do its work. The claims go like
this: Christians played only one among many roles in the
founding of the United States. Many of the founders were
Enlightenment-style deists. The founders distrusted religion. They feared Europe's experience with established
churches and wars of religion. Thomas Jefferson supported a "wall of separation" between church and state.
He wanted to keep religion from wrecking the reasonable
order of civil affairs.

And anyway, times have changed. Today, the United
States has many religions. The faith of one group of citizens always tends to offend or victimize some other
group. A pluralistic society can't afford a dominant idea
of God. Religious belief is too diverse. To avoid sectarian
warfare, we need to keep religion out of the national public conversation. The state stands above moral and religious tribalism. It can best ensure the rights of everyone.
Thus, a fully secularized public life would be the adult-
hood of the American experiment; a place where mature
citizens and leaders could put aside private obsessions to
choose the best course for the widest public. Or so the argument goes.

Of course, nations do in fact change over time. Their

public institutions must adjust. The United States is larger and more diverse than it was two hundred years ago. We face many new challenges. But unless we solve our problems in a way consistent with our founding beliefs and principles, we will become a very different nation. American identity as a nation is not built on ethnicity. It comes from a specific, religiously informed understanding of the world and human nature, and the convictions that derive from this understanding. This is where the effort to exclude religious faith from the discussion of public issues is so damaging and often so dishonest.

Evidence for the Christian role in founding and shaping the United States is so massive that denying it requires a peculiar kind of self-deception. As the historian Paul Johnson observes, "America was born Protestant." He adds that "it is important to grasp that American society embraced the principles of voluntarism and tolerance in [religious] faith in a spirit not of secularism, but of piety." The United States was never imagined, therefore, as "a secular state; it might more accurately be described as a moral and ethical society without a state religion."[41]

Many of our key political documents, like Abraham Lincoln's second inaugural address, the Declaration of Independence, and even the Virginia Statute for Religious Freedom drafted by Thomas Jefferson himself, would fail the test pushed by today's secularizers. Religious language underpins them all. More importantly, religious conviction frames their reasoning.

Secular is a slippery word. In its original meaning, it simply refers to being in or of the world. Catholics who join "secular institutes" don't leave the church. Rather, they bind themselves together in small communities to live their faith more deeply while working *in the world.* When the church talks about the "secular clergy," it means the diocesan priests and deacons who serve the lay Catholic faithful in parishes.

But in modern use, *secular* often takes on an ugly meaning. Today's secularist agenda assumes that religion is, at best, otherworldly. At worst, religion is irrational and dangerous. This perspective ignores Christianity's formative role in American life. It also demeans the intelligence and goodwill of millions of American believers with paranoia about "Christocrats" and theocracy. The specter of an American theocracy is a tool designed to bully serious religious believers into silence.

Americans have always believed in *nonsectarian* public institutions. But the founders never intended a nation that privatizes religion and excludes it from involvement in public affairs. Nor did they create any such nation. The secularism proposed today for our public life is not religion-neutral. It is *antireligious.* It implies that the key qualities of Christianity and other major religions are division and extremism. In the light of U.S. history, it's hard to imagine a more alien idea. The American experiment is the product of religiously shaped vocabulary, thought, and tradition. It can't be sustained without respecting the living roots of that vocabulary.

A truly secularized United States would be a country without a soul; a nation with a hole in its chest. Such a state could not stand above tribalism in public affairs. It would become a tool of the strongest tribe. American belief in the sanctity of individual rights depends on a God who guarantees those rights, and to whom the state is subordinate and responsible. And this view is not an opinion. It is the historical *fact* that provided the foundation for the rest of our public life.

Secularism as a cult—the kind of rigid separationism where the state treats religion as a scary and unstable guest—hollows out the core of what it means to be human. It treats the most important part of life, the moral and religious, as a private quirk. It starves a nation's spirit. And it has never been a natural step toward democratic maturity. The rise of American secularism did not occur by chance. It didn't happen inevitably as a result of modern progress. As Christian Smith and other scholars have chronicled, it came about through the intentional political struggle of secularizing activists in education, science, the media, and the law.[42]

Of course, turnabout is fair play. Believers can push back.

• • •

ABOUT 90 PERCENT of Americans believe in God. About 80 percent describe themselves as Christians. Nearly three-quarters pray at least once a week. Nearly half attend religious services at least once a month. It's a matter of record that Americans are a religious people.[43] It's also true that the Christian faith is the dominant religious influence on the American soul. Many millions of Americans not only claim to be Christian but also actively practice their faith. But what this means for their public witness is less clear and also less reassuring.

Nearly 61 percent of Americans believe a presidential candidate should be a religious person. Clear majorities of both Republican and Democratic voters feel that religion is vital in their own lives. More than half of Americans polled describe themselves as very religious.[44] Compared to the figures for Europe, these numbers are astounding. But Americans also have a deeply anti-institutional streak deriving from their Protestant roots, including a distrust of *religious* institutions. It's also true, according to the researcher George Barna, that American theological views have veered away in recent years from classical scriptural beliefs. Some 66 percent of Americans believe in an omnipotent, all-knowing God who rules creation. But this is the lowest recorded number in more than two decades of studies.

As Barna notes, "Americans are willing to expend some energy in religious activities such as attending church and reading the Bible, and they are willing to throw some money in the offering basket. Because of such activities, they convince themselves that they are a people of genuine faith. But when it comes to truly establishing their priorities and making a tangible commitment to knowing and loving God, and to allowing Him to change their character and lifestyle, most people stop short. We want to be 'spiritual' and we want to have God's favor, but we're not sure we want Him taking control of our lives and messing with the image and outcomes we've worked so hard to produce."[45]

It's hard to see this as anything but a case of split personality. In practice, we've buried ourselves in material pursuits, distractions, and what Neil Postman once described as technological narcotics.[46] Early Christians would have called it something even worse: *acedia*; a stagnancy or sloth of the soul that shows itself in an unwillingness to "judge" in the name of false compassion; a disregard for moral conviction that hides behind flexibility and openness.

If our nation has changed from the land of opportunity to the land of private appetites over the last few decades, one of the reasons is this: *We haven't lived what we say we believe.* Homelessness, poverty, abortion, the exploitation of undocumented immigrants, the neglect of the elderly—these are brazenly real problems in contemporary America. They won't go away by blaming the Religious Right, smearing Christian believers as extremists, or kicking religion out of the public discussion. That's the language of a power grab by people alienated from our country's religious roots.

Our problems can only be solved by people of character who *actively and without apology* take their beliefs into public debates. That includes Catholics. We need to be stronger in our public witness, not weaker. Whether America is really 80 percent or 50 percent or 10 percent Christian doesn't matter. If we really believe that Jesus Christ is who he says he is, and that the Catholic Church is who *she* says she is, then we need to live like it. If we really believe that the Gospel is true, we need to embody it in our private lives and our public choices.

In the end, we can choose to be the small, hollow "men without chests" that C. S. Lewis described in *The Abolition of Man*: people who have plenty of comforts but no greatness of soul; a contented and conditioned herd without courage, purpose, nobility, or conviction. We can ignore the historian Christopher Dawson when he warned, "This is the greatest misery of modern civilization—that it has conquered the world by losing its own soul, and when its soul is lost, it must lose the world as well."[47]

Or we can choose to be the people God created us to be. But of course, that raises the question of why we're here.

3.

WHY WE'RE HERE

MAN'S SEARCH FOR MEANING is one of the most widely read books of the last century. But nobody should be surprised. Asked about his book's enormous success, Viktor Frankl answered that he didn't see it as a personal achievement. Instead, he felt it was testimony to the misery of our age. If millions of people seek out a book, he said, whose very title promises to deal with the question of life's meaning, then it must be a question "that burns under their fingernails."[1]

Much of Frankl's book is autobiographical. It deals with his experiences as a Jewish prisoner in Nazi death camps during World War II. Over the course of his ordeal, he watched some physically strong men give up and die while other, much weaker men survived. The difference, he discovered, is this: When a man believes that he has a future, when he believes in a reason to go on living, he is much more likely to survive. When he doesn't, he dies.

For Frankl, a moment came, marching in the snow with other prisoners, cursed and kicked by guards, when he remembered the image of his wife with a clarity "more luminous than the sun that was beginning to rise." A thought occurred to him for the first time in his life: "that love is the ultimate and highest goal to which man can aspire." And in that instant, "I grasped the meaning of the greatest secret that human poetry and human thought and belief have to impart: *The salvation of man is through love and in love.*"[2]

Frankl's words seem to have a special weight for Catholics. Christianity, more than any other religion, orders itself around love. Both John Paul II and Benedict XVI lived through the same Nazi era that Frankl did. Rather than lose their faith, both men found it more deeply. Like Frankl, both men chose to anchor their lives in love rather than in hate. As a result, John Paul II—the child of a nation crushed by two totalitarian regimes in a row—could still preach that love is the "fundamental and innate vocation" of every human being.[3] This vocation (or "calling," from the Latin verb *vocare*) is the heart of the Christian faith. Catholics believe that each human life has a unique but interrelated meaning. We are created by the God who is the source of love itself; a God who loved the world so fiercely that he sent his only Son to redeem it.

In other words, we were made by Love, to receive love ourselves, and *to show love to others.* That's why we're here. That's our purpose. And it has very practical consequences—including the political kind.

The Christian mission in the world comes from the nature of God himself. Catholics believe in one God. But he is a God in three Persons sharing one nature. This belief is not just an exercise in theology. It's central to Catholic life. It gives a framework to all Christian thought and action. For Catholics, God is a living community of love—Father, Son, and Holy Spirit—and in creating us, God intends us to take part in that community of mutual giving. All of Christian life comes down to sharing in the exchange of love within the heart of the Trinity and then offering that love to others in our relationships.

For Christians, reality is grounded in *both* unity and plurality. Personhood, whether we mean the Persons of the Trinity or our human person, is always bound up with relationship. God is eternal and unchanging, but he is not static. Within the life of the Trinity, there are the Trinitarian missions of the Father loving the Son, the Son loving the Father, and the Holy Spirit proceeding from the love between Father and Son—and all human beings have a mission in the world that reflects that divine love and takes part in that exchange.

Of course, these are nice ideas. Anyone can give them a pious nod. Even many Catholics mouth the word *love* without a clue to what it really implies. This is why so much of modern Christian life seems like a bad version of a mediocre Beatles song rather than the morning of Pentecost. For a Christian, love is not simply an emotion. Feelings pass. They're fickle, and they often lie. Real love is an act of the will; a sustained choice that proves itself not just by what we say but by *what we do.*

A man may claim he loves his wife. His wife will want to see the evidence. In like manner, we can talk about God all we please, but God will not be fooled. Jesus told the story of the sheep and the goats (Matthew 25:31–46) for a reason. Saying we're Catholic does not mean we are, except in the thinnest sense. Relationships have consequences in actions. Otherwise, they're just empty words. Our relationship with God is no exception. When Jesus asks Peter, "Do you love me?" and Peter answers yes, it's no surprise that Jesus immediately follows up with: "Then feed my sheep" (John 21:17).* God loves us always. We can choose to ignore that. All of the damned do. But if we claim to love *him,* it's an "if/then" kind of deal, with obligations of conduct and personal honesty just like any good marriage or friendship.

The twist in loving God is that it's not a standard "I, Thou" affair. It turns out to be an "I, Thou—and everybody else" kind of arrangement. Christian faith is not just vertical. It's also horizontal. Since God created all human persons and guarantees their dignity by his Fa-

*Biblical quotations are from the Ignatius Revised Standard Version Bible, 2nd edition (San Francisco: Ignatius Press, 2003).

therhood, we have family duties to one another. That applies especially within the *ekklesia*—the community of believers we call the church—but it extends to the whole world. This means our faith has social as well as personal implications. And those social implications include the civil dimension of our shared life; in other words, the content of our politics.

For Christians, love is a small word that relentlessly unpacks into a lot of other words: *truth, repentance, forgiveness, mercy, charity, courage, justice.* These are action words, all of them, including *truth,* because in accepting Jesus Christ, the Gospel says that we will know the truth, and the truth *will make us free* (John 8:32)—not comfortable; not respected; but *free* in the real sense of the word: able to see and do what's right. This freedom is meant to be used in the service of others. Working for justice is an obligation of Christian freedom. Saint Augustine wrote that the state not governed by justice is no more than a gang of thieves. Thus, it's here, in the search for justice, that the Catholic citizen engages the political world because, as Benedict XVI says, "justice is both the aim and the intrinsic criterion of all politics." In fact, the just ordering of society and the state "is the central responsibility of politics."[4]

Christians in general and Catholics in particular do not, and should not, seek to "force" their religious beliefs on society. But working to form the public conscience is not coercion any more than teaching the difference between poison and a steak is a form of bullying. Actively witnessing to and advancing what we believe to be true about key moral issues in public life is not "coercion." It's honesty. And it's also a duty—not only of faith but of citizenship.

The philosopher Friedrich Nietzsche once famously claimed that God is dead, and we have killed him. He despised Christianity as a slave morality. But he had an oddly divided view of Christ himself: admiring Jesus for his genius and strength; but at the same time reviling him for choosing to be the receptacle of other people's sins.

Nietzsche was wrong about the real nature of Christian faith, but we do need to consider what he said. Jesus accepted every measure of suffering on the cross. He did it freely. He *chose* it. The Father made this sacrifice for us through his Son because he loves us. There is nothing weak or cowardly or life-denying about *that* kind of radical love—and any parent who has suffered along with a dying child instinctively knows it. The question we need to ask ourselves, if we call ourselves Christians today, is this: Do we *really* want to follow Jesus Christ and love as he did, or is it just too inconvenient? We can choose differently. We can choose the kind of routine, self-absorbed, halfhearted, anesthetic Christianity for which Nietzsche had such contempt. It's certainly easier. It also costs less.

. . .

A FRIEND OF mine tells a story from the 1950s. His parents were driving from New York to Texas with his younger sister and himself to visit family. They stopped on a Sunday morning in a small town in Alabama to get gas. His father asked the station attendant where they could find a local Catholic church. "No Catholic church here," shrugged the attendant. "No Catholics in the county." His father paid for the gas, they pulled out of the gas station, turned the corner, and there, half a block down the street, was the local Catholic parish.

Many Catholics have grown up in recent decades with no memory of the often vulgar and sometimes violent anti-Catholicism that pervades American history. Anti-Catholic bigotry in the United States traces itself back to the country's original Protestant roots. Fortunately, much of the old, religiously based anti-Catholicism has softened since the 1950s, and some of this change surely flows from Catholic ecumenical and reform efforts since Vatican II. Over the past forty years, Catholics and other committed Christians have found that they have much more in common, and much more to feel commonly uneasy about in the wider culture, than in the past. This is a good thing.

Anti-Catholicism has not gone away, though. It has only shifted its shape. The new anti-Catholicism is a kind of background radiation to daily life created by America's secularized leadership classes: the media, the academy, and political action groups. Some of the bigotry is very direct. It worries publicly about the Catholic faith of U.S. Supreme Court justices. Or it lobbies the Internal Revenue Service to attack the tax status of Catholic organizations that teach an inconvenient public message.

But a lot of the new bigotry simply involves a steady stress on Catholic sins while turning a blind eye to Catholic vitality. It also includes a great many pious lectures about not imposing Catholic beliefs on society. In reality, the new anti-Catholicism often masks a resentment of *any* faithful Christian social engagement. Nonetheless, the Catholic Church in the United States makes an ideal target for critics of religion in the public square because we're larger and better organized than most other Christian communities. And thanks to habits of mind created by the "old" anti-Catholicism, Catholics are easier to caricature.

In a democracy, people disagree. It's a natural part of the process, but disagreement can easily create resentment. And when people act together in community, resentment of their ideas can fester into hatred of who they are. The reason is simple. It's usually easy to ignore individuals, but communities are another matter. When organized and focused communities—like the Catholic Church—are pressing for what they believe, they are much stronger and much harder to ignore than are individuals.

What many critics dislike most about the Catholic Church is not her message, which they can always choose to dismiss, but her *institutional coherence* in pursuing her message, which is much harder to push aside. And yet the church is neither a religious version of General Motors nor a "political" organism; the political consequences of her message are a by-product of her *moral* teachings.

The church—both as a community and as an "institution"—is vital to Catholic life. Catholics believe that the church is the Body of Christ, the community of believers formed by the Holy Spirit to continue Jesus' work until he returns. The church is a family of different but equal people, gathered in a hierarchy of authority with Christ as the head and a mission to sanctify the world. The church is also, in a sense, a *person*—our mother and teacher; the spouse of Christ. This is why Catholics so often refer to the church as a "she." The community of faith is essentially *feminine*—not passive or weak, but fertile with new life. Mary cooperated with God in making his Word incarnate. In the same way the church, in following Christ, creates new life in the world through the faith and works of her children.

The church engages the world in two ways: through the life of each individual believer and through the common action of believers working together. Every Christian life, and every choice in every Christian life, *matters.* There's no special headquarters staff that handles the action side of the Gospel. That task belongs to all of us. Baptism, for Catholics, does not simply wash away sin. It also incorporates the baptized person into a new life; and part of that new life is a mandate to act; to be God's agent in the world. Laypeople, clergy, and religious all have different tasks within the community of faith. *Everybody,* however, shares the basic mission: bringing Jesus Christ to the world, and the world to Jesus Christ.

Laypeople have the special task of evangelizing the secular world. And this makes sense. Most Catholics— the vast majority—are laypeople. They have jobs, friends, and families. They can witness Jesus Christ on a daily basis, silently or out loud, directly or indirectly, by their words and actions. If we look for opportunities to share our faith with others, God always provides them. This is why self-described Catholics who live so anonymously that no one knows about their faith, Catholics who fail to prove by their actions what they claim to believe with their tongue, aren't really living as "Catholics" at all.

It's also why asking Catholics to keep their faith out of public affairs amounts to telling them to be barren; to behave as if they were neutered. Nothing could be more alien to the meaning of baptism. The Christian idea of witness, which comes from the Greek word *martyr,* isn't limited to a bloody death in the arena for the faith. *All* Christians have the command to be a martyr in the public arena—to live a life of conscious witness wherever God places them, no matter how insignificant it seems and whether or not they ever see the results.

Years ago I read a story about an Englishwoman

named Mabel. She had two sons. It's not clear what first drew her to the Gospel, but she became a Christian shortly after her husband died in the 1890s. She was devoted to her new faith. Every Sunday she would make the long walk with her sons to an Anglican church. Then one Sunday they tried a different place of worship: a Catholic church in a poor area of Birmingham. Mabel already had an interest in things Catholic. She asked for instruction. She then entered the Catholic Church.

Mabel's Catholic conversion angered her family. Her father was outraged. Her brother-in-law ended the little financial help he had been giving her since she became a widow. Her dead husband's family rejected her. She and her sons slipped into poverty. Mabel's health collapsed. Despite this, she remained zealously committed to her Catholic faith and taught it to both her sons. Several years later, she fell into a diabetes-induced coma and died. She entrusted her boys to the guardianship of a friend, a local Catholic priest, who deepened their faith throughout their upbringing.[5]

Very few people remember Mabel and her story. But a great many people remember at least one of her sons: J. R. R. Tolkien. In a letter to a Jesuit friend many years later, Tolkien wrote: "All my own small perception of beauty both in majesty and simplicity is founded" on Mary, the mother of Jesus, and that "*The Lord of the Rings* is of course a fundamentally religious and Catholic work." He added, "[My Catholic faith has] nourished me

and taught me all the little that I know; and t
to my mother, who clung to her conversion
young, largely through the hardships of povert
ing from it."[6]

That's not a bad epitaph for any Christian life. It also
reminds us that real discipleship always has a cost. We
can't follow Jesus Christ without sharing in his cross.
That requires humility and courage because it can hurt.
Quite a few people in the modern world dismiss Christ:
some quietly; some with loud derision; and if they hate
him, they will also hate his church and his followers—at
least the ones who seek to follow him in their actions as
well as their words.

The word *disciple*, after all, comes from the Latin
word meaning learner, student, or pupil. A good student
learns from and emulates his or her teacher. Discipleship
demands more than reading about the Catholic faith or
admiring the life of Jesus. Christ didn't ask for our approval or agreement. He doesn't need either. He asked us
to *follow* him—radically, with all we have, and without
caveats or reservations.

Following Christ means paying the same price out of
love for others that Jesus paid to redeem us. Following
Christ means working for justice in civil society in the
light of Christian truth; it means treating the persons we
meet every day with charity. Christ's call to follow him
applies to each of us as individual believers. It also applies to the whole community we call the church.

As the Lutheran pastor Dietrich Bonhoeffer wrote from prison in 1944, "I've come to know more and more the profound this-worldliness of Christianity . . . I don't mean the shallow and banal this-worldliness of the enlightened, the busy, the comfortable or the lascivious, but the profound this-worldliness characterized by discipline and the constant knowledge of death and resurrection."[7] We remember Bonhoeffer for his books like *Life Together* and *The Cost of Discipleship.* But we remember him even more for another reason. He paid the cost of his discipleship personally. He was hanged by the Third Reich in 1945 for his part in resistance activities.

We Christians are in the world but not of the world. We belong to God, and our home is heaven. But we're here for a reason: to *change* the world, *for the sake of* the world, in the name of Jesus Christ. The work belongs to us. Nobody will do it for us. And the idea that we can accomplish it without engaging in a hands-on way the laws, the structures, the public policies, the habits of mind, and the root causes that sustain injustice in our country is a delusion.

SOMEONE ONCE ASKED me how any sensible person could choose to become a Christian because Christians have such an unhealthy desire for suffering. The best answer comes from Léon Bloy, a writer who himself chose to become a Catholic. "Man has places in his heart which do not yet exist," wrote Bloy, "and into them enters suffering, that they might have existence."[8] In a sense, all Christian belief is cocooned in those words. Christians have no desire to suffer. But we do understand and appreciate the power of suffering. No one can avoid suffering. It's the truest democratic experience. Everybody gets a piece of it. But Bloy understood, just as Viktor Frankl discovered in the death camps, that we can always choose what we do with the suffering that comes our way. We have that freedom. This is why suffering breaks some people, while it *breaks open* others into something more than their old selves, stretching the soul to greatness.

Christians don't like suffering any more than anyone else. They certainly don't go looking for it. But people who believe in Jesus Christ do try to accept and use suffering as Christ did: that is, as a creative, redemptive act. Suffering lived properly is the heart's great tutor in humility, gratitude, and understanding of others, because they too suffer. This is why Pope John Paul II once described the Bible as the "great book about suffering."[9] He meant that Scripture is the story of God's willingness to suffer for humanity; the story of God's call to each of us to join our suffering to his own in healing the evil and pain in the world. Scripture urges us to follow the Good Samaritan who saw even a suffering stranger as his neighbor and acted to ease his wounds. Thus God's "great book

·ing" is not only about God's love for us—but
)ur *solidarity with others.* The cornerstone for
.... action in the world is the Word of God itself.

Catholics believe that Scripture is the infallible
Word of God. They *also* remember that the church
teaches with the authority of Jesus by Christ's own command, and that the church preceded the Gospels—not
the other way around. The Christian community is
shaped by both Scripture and Tradition. The New Testament was written in context and by members of the
ekklesia, the early Christian church. As the true Word of
God, the Scriptures always stand in judgment of the
present Christian community. Being faithful to God depends on whether we live our individual lives and our life
in the church in accord with Scripture.

But again, the Scriptures come to us from God
through the church. So an intrinsic relationship flows between Word and believing community from the very
start of the Christian experience. This is the meaning of
Tradition. For Catholics, Tradition is the wisdom learned
from the lived experience of the church applying God's
Word to the circumstances of the day. The Word of God
is foundational to Christian life. It judges Christian life.
But other dimensions of Christian life also exist side by
side with Scripture, notably our life together in Jesus
Christ as a believing community, passed on through the
centuries.

Here's the point. We can't reject the church and her

teachings, and then simultaneously claim to be following Jesus Christ or the Scriptures. For Catholics, the believing community *is the church*, and without the church as the guardian of Christian life and protector of God's Word, Christianity could never have survived. As the historian Christopher Dawson wrote, "Christianity was not merely a doctrine and a life, it was above all a society." Without the framework of the church, "Christianity would have changed its nature in [history's] changing social environment and would have become . . . a different religion."[10]

Why is any of this important in talking about Catholics, politics, and the public square? It should be obvious. The believing community—the church—is how the individual believer brings the Word of God and the body of Christian wisdom most forcefully to bear on the practical affairs of the world. And that can thoroughly irritate the world and also Caesar, whether the year is AD 112, 1012, or 2012.

Catholic public engagement comes from the same religiously informed roots that gave life to the ideas and words of America's founders more than two hundred years ago. As Dietrich Bonhoeffer wrote from the distance of Nazi Germany, "American democracy is founded not upon the emancipated man but, quite the contrary, upon the kingdom of God and upon the limitation of all earthly powers by the sovereignty of God."[11] Christianity requires faith in things unseen. It points the individual person toward eternal life with God. But our salvation is worked out here and now, together as a family, in *this* world, through our actions toward other people. For a Christian, this world is worth struggling to make better—precisely because God created it and loves his children who inhabit it.

Thus, it's no surprise that in the Decalogue, the first three commandments frame humanity's relationship with God. The next seven frame our relationship with each other. The desire for extending God's justice among his people, marked by the Old Testament tradition of Jubilee in Leviticus 25 or the warnings in the Book of Amos, weaves itself throughout the New Testament. When asked to name the greatest commandment in the law, Jesus answered: "You shall love the Lord your God with all your heart, and with all your soul, and with all your mind. This is the great and first commandment. And a second is like it. You shall love your neighbor as yourself. On these two commandments depend all the law and all the prophets" (Matthew 22:37–40). What that love means in practice can be found in the words Jesus used to describe his true disciples: *leaven in the world, salt of the earth, light to the nations.* These are words of mission; a language not of good intentions but of conscious *behavior.*

The Epistle of James describes the meaning of discipleship best when it warns Christians to "be doers of the Word and not hearers only, deceiving yourselves" (1:22) and that "faith by itself, if it has no works, is dead" (2:17). That message incarnates itself down through the centuries in the lives of saints, religious orders, social encyclicals, and a vast tradition of Catholic hospitals, schools, and services to the hungry, disabled, poor, homeless, and elderly. When emperor Julian the Apostate sought to restore Roman paganism in the fourth century AD, he didn't copy Christian thought. He had contempt for what Christians believed. Instead he copied Christian hospices, orphanages, and other charitable works because of their power to witness by action. But if faith without works is dead, so too in the long run are *works* dead without a dynamic faith to grow and sustain them. Christians had that faith. Pagan Roman culture didn't. The rest is history.

As Catholics, how can we uncouple what we *do*, from what we claim to *believe*, without killing what we believe and lying in what we do? The answer is simple. We can't. How we act works backward on our convictions, making them stronger or smothering them under a snowfall of alibis.

To German Catholics of the politically desperate 1930s, Pope Pius XI wrote, "It is not enough to be a member of the Church of Christ; one needs to be a living member in spirit and in truth, i.e., living in the state of grace and in the presence of God, either in innocence or sincere repentance."[12] He warned that "what is morally indefensible can never contribute to the good of the people,"[13] and that "thousands of voices ring in your ears a [false] gospel which has not been revealed by the Father of heaven."[14] Too few Catholics listened. In fact, far too many German Christians—including too many church leaders—accommodated themselves to a Caesar who took their souls along with their approval.

Parallels between Europe seventy years ago and the American landscape today may seem glib and melodramatic, or even flatly wrong. It's a fair criticism. Times change. History never really repeats itself. Each generation has its own unique set of challenges. But patterns of human thought and behavior *do* repeat themselves. The past, as a record of the results, is a great teacher. When John Paul II called Catholics to a purification of memory and repentance for sins of the past during the Jubilee Year 2000, he did it for an important reason. We can't preach what we don't live. The struggle with our own sinfulness never ends in this lifetime, but we must at least admit our sins, repent of them, seek the forgiveness of those we wound—and then constantly begin again.

As Reinhold Niebuhr wrote, "No Christian Church has a right to preach to this so-called secular age without a contrite recognition of the shortcomings of historic Christianity which tempted the modern age to disavow its Christian faith." The unbelief of the modern heart is not simply a product of human pride. It can also be what

Niebuhr called a "reaction to [the] profanity" of faith lived hypocritically.[15]

What that means for the church and individual American Catholics is this: We can choose to treat our faith as a collection of comforting pieties. We can choose to file Jesus away as a good teacher with some great, if unrealistic, ideas. Or we can choose to be real disciples, despite all our sins and *admitting* all our sins. In other words, we can accept Jesus for who he says he is: our redeemer, the Messiah of Israel, and the only Son of God. This is what the church has always believed. What we *can't* honestly choose is continuing to select our Catholic faith from a cafeteria menu while failing at the task Christ himself gave us: a root-level transformation of *ourselves and the world around us.* The time for easy Christianity is over. In fact, it never really existed. We're blessed to be rid of the illusion. We need to be more zealous in our faith, not more discreet; clearer in our convictions, not muddier; and *more* Catholic, not less.

The Catholic faith should take root in our hearts like the mustard seed of Jesus' parables (Matthew 13:31; 17:20). No matter how small it begins, the mustard seed grows so strong and so large that it breaks us open and frees us to be new and different persons far better than our old selves; a source of shelter and support for others. The one thing we can't do with a living faith is remain the same. We must either kill it or become new people because of it. Anything less is fraud. And in like manner,

the church should be a mustard seed in society, transforming—not by coercion but by active witness—every
fiber of a nation's political, economic, and social life.

History reminds us that believers and their leaders
are as prone to the temptations of power as anyone else.
Jesus himself turned away from earthly power when Satan offered it to him on the mountain (Matthew 4:8–10).
God's kingdom is not of this world. Nothing we can do
will change that. Even a good Caesar is still only Caesar.

But Christ never absolved us from resisting and healing the evil in the world, or from solidarity with the people who suffer it. Our fidelity is finally to God, but it
implies a faithfulness to the needs of his creation. Like it
or not, we are *involved*—and there is, after all, a war on
(Ephesians 6:12). It's the same conflict Tolkien meant
when he wrote that "[human] wars are always lost, and
The War always goes on."[16] It's the same conflict C. S.
Lewis meant when he wrote that "there is no neutral
ground in the universe; every square inch, every split second, is claimed by God and counter-claimed by Satan."[17]
And this war goes on without rest in *every* age, in *every* nation, in *every* human life, in every choice, in every decision, in every action, in every public issue.

We can choose our side. We can't choose not to
choose. Not choosing is a choice.

4.

CONSTANTINE'S CHILDREN

LET'S BEGIN WITH A story. We'll call it "a tale of two bishops."

Archbishop Joseph Rummel served the Catholic people of New Orleans from 1935 until his death in 1964. By the 1950s, he faced an increasingly ugly problem. The Archdiocese of New Orleans had the largest Catholic population in the Deep South and many thousands of black Catholics. It also had segregated schools. Rummel and previous bishops had always ensured that black students had access to Catholic education. However, segregated parochial schools had the same scarce money and poor quality as the segregated public schools.

After World War II, Rummel began desegregating the local church. In 1948, his seminary welcomed two black students. In 1951, Rummel pulled the White and Colored signs from Catholic parishes. In 1953, a year before the U.S. Supreme Court struck down segregation in public schools, he issued the first of two strong pastoral letters: *Blessed Are the Peacemakers.* Pastors read it to their people at every Mass one Sunday. In it, Rummel condemned segregation. It drew a quick response. Some parishioners bitterly resented hearing from the pulpit that "there will be no further discrimination or segregation in the pews, at the Communion rail, at the confessional and in parish meetings, just as there will be no segregation in the kingdom of heaven."

In 1956, Rummel said he intended to desegregate Catholic schools. Tempers ran hot. Most parish school boards voted against desegregation. Rummel didn't budge. A year earlier, he had closed a parish when its people objected to their newly assigned black priest. But to compound the archbishop's troubles, many parents had moved their children from public to Catholic schools, hoping to avoid desegregation. Members of the Louisiana legislature threatened to withhold then-available public funds for Catholic schools if Rummel went ahead with his plans.

In early 1962, Rummel said that in the following year, Catholic schools would integrate. Several Catholic politicians organized public protests and letter-writing campaigns. They threatened a boycott of Catholic schools. On April 16, 1962, Rummel excommunicated three prominent Catholics—a judge, a political writer, and a community organizer—for publicly defying the teaching of their church.

The New Orleans events made national news, covered by *Time* magazine and the *New York Times*. The *Times* editorial board gushed that "men of all faiths must admire [Rummel's] unwavering courage" because he has "set an example founded on religious principle and is responsive to the social conscience of our time."[1]

In 2004, another archbishop, Raymond Burke of St. Louis, drew national headlines. In his final weeks as bishop of La Crosse, Wisconsin, he asked three Catholic public figures to refrain from presenting themselves for Communion. He then asked his priests to withhold Communion from Catholic public officials who supported abortion rights. The three offending politicians claimed merely to be pro-choice. In Burke's view, though, their actions showed a material support for abortion and a stubborn disregard for their own faith. All three had voted for or otherwise supported forcing Catholic hospitals to provide abortions. In effect, they had publicly tried to coerce the church to violate her teaching on a serious sanctity-of-life issue.

Burke's action, though softer than Rummel's, made him quite a few enemies, even among people who saw themselves as Catholic. Unlike Rummel, Burke received no glowing praise from the *New York Times*. He got rather different treatment from the news media. But again like Rummel, he hadn't checked with the *Times* for its approval. What the *Times* thought didn't matter. What the church believed, did.

The moral of our story is this: First, when Catholics

take their church seriously and act on her teaching in the world, somebody, and often somebody with power, won't like it. Second, in recent American politics, the line that divides "prophetic witness" from "violating the separation of church and state" usually depends on who draws the line, who gets offended—and by what issue. The line wanders conveniently. But Catholics, in seeking to live their faith, can't follow convenience.

THOMAS JEFFERSON ONCE described the teaching of history as a central purpose of education. The Greek writer Thucydides saw history as a guide to interpreting the future. And Niccolò Machiavelli, one of history's shrewdest political thinkers, wrote, "Whoever wishes to foresee the future must consult the past; for human events ever resemble those of preceding times."

Knowing history *matters*. In fact, it's vital to American political life. If we don't understand the past, we can't make sense of the present. Nor can we build a healthy future. Unfortunately, many American Catholics tend to forget the role the church has played throughout history in shaping the public square. Due to that ignorance, they often accept a bad version of their own story. Over the past three hundred years, critics from Voltaire to Christopher Hitchens have castigated the church as a barrier to human progress. This is simply false. The record of history shows *why* it is false. If we accept a narrative of our own story written by skeptics of the Christian faith, we are not being "open" or balanced. We are colluding in a lie.

What the mass media thought about Joseph Rummel in 1962 or Raymond Burke in 2004 may be interesting. It is also irrelevant. It has nothing to do with the rightness of either man's actions. Excommunication and withholding Communion are serious matters. Good people can disagree about the prudence of such actions in specific circumstances. Nevertheless, Catholics who know their faith also know that publicly opposing racism and publicly opposing abortion flow from the same Catholic beliefs about the dignity of the human person. Both evils are inexcusably wrong. On matters like these, the church has the duty to teach the world—not the reverse.

Catholic teaching often has political side effects because it has *public* implications. In every age, Christians have faced a new version of the same dilemma: They need to act fruitfully in the world without being absorbed by it. They need to love the world for the right reasons and in the right way: that is, because *God* loves it and seeks its salvation. As we've already seen, the dynamic tension in Christian life comes from the two great commandments. We should love God above everything else; and because of that, we should love the people he created as we love ourselves. We must seek God first; but we can't reach him without living lives of justice and mercy in relationship to other people, here and now.

This paradox has always tempted Christians in at least two mistaken directions. The first leads to a kind of fatalism. We treat our faith as a purely private relationship with God. The logic goes like this: The world is a fallen place. It's also very complicated. Jesus himself said the poor would always be with us. If he couldn't fix their problems, neither can we. Getting our hands dirty in the practical clay of too many human affairs can smear mud all over our piety. The state is a creature of this practical clay. It is either unrelated to the task of salvation or a potential obstacle to it. In any event, we Christians have no final home here. We're just passing through.

The second mistaken direction, less common in our day, leads to seeing the world as a subordinate order to the church. The reasoning goes like this: If God created the world, it belongs to him. Christ gave the church the mandate to continue his work of salvation. The church is the bride of Christ and therefore speaks for God. It follows then that religious authority should trump secular authority even in purely temporal matters.

These are very broad strokes. History is far more complex than anyone can distill in a few sentences. Still, we can see where these impulses might end. The first can result in a Christian withdrawal from the world; an avoidance of personal and community engagement with the real problems of society. Where the second impulse leads is even clearer from past events. Lord Acton's warning that power tends to corrupt, and absolute power corrupts absolutely, can apply just as easily to religious leaders as to their political counterparts.

The official mingling of church and state—Europe's classic "altar and throne" arrangements of the past—arose from late Roman history and gradually developed into medieval Christendom, which helped frame the civilization we have today. Over the centuries, this often led to a confusion of secular and religious spheres. As a result, the church learned, through long and often bitter experience, the limits of a healthy relationship with the state. Today, as we reexamine the borders between civil and religious authority, one of the most important tasks facing American Catholics is *remembering* that history.

That can be hard in America, and not just for Catholics. Christopher Lasch once observed that Americans know so little history not because they lack the skills to learn it, but because they don't *want* to know it. The industrialist Henry Ford captured this American mood when he said: "History is more or less bunk. It's tradition. We don't want tradition. We want to live in the present, and the only history that is worth a tinker's damn is the history that we make today." In fact, when Americans consider the past at all, they usually prefer nostalgia—the soft-focus version of the past that serves as a kind of entertainment. Americans, Lasch argued, dislike real history because the past, as it actually happened, places irritating limits on the present and the future. It restricts our possibilities. We can't reinvent ourselves today if we're dragging around a true record of what happened yesterday.[2]

The danger in indulging this strange American habit is that we develop a kind of amnesia. Persons with amnesia lose more than their memory. They also lose their identity. A man with amnesia may accept nearly any story about his past, no matter how misleading, as true. The same applies to nations and communities—and also to churches. This is why recovering the past accurately has practical *political* consequences for Catholics in the present.

FOR CHRISTIANS, BICKERING over the "separation of church and state" isn't new. It has very long roots.

The emperor Constantine the Great ended the Roman persecution of Christians in AD 313 with the Edict of Milan. In doing so, he began the remaking of the ancient world. Before Constantine, Christians made up a steadily growing minority in the Roman Empire. But in the century after his death, in one of history's most rapid shifts, millions converted to the new faith. Within a few decades, Christianity had become the official state religion. Christian worship and thought suffused late Roman civilization. In the aftermath of this one man and his embrace of Christianity, the rudder of human events seemed to turn.

Much of Eastern Christianity regards Constantine as a saint. His mother, Helena, was a woman of deep Christian piety, and Constantine revered her. Secular scholars take a more complicated view of his religious motives. Some argue that he decriminalized and then favored the Christian faith in order to cement his power and unify a fractured empire. It's certainly true that Constantine was both visionary and ruthless. He had no trouble killing his opponents, including a son and a nephew. He also delayed his baptism until late in life. Nevertheless, most evidence suggests that he was sincere in his religious belief. As ruler, he clearly saw himself as anointed by God with a sacred role equal and parallel to bishops in the church. He intervened often and sometimes for the better in the disputes of the young Christian community. The first ecumenical council—the Council of Nicaea, which played a vital role in codifying Christian belief— was called by Constantine.

Constantine's influence on later Christian history, however, has often caused debate within the church herself. In fact for some, his legacy is a very mixed blessing. Knowing the reasons for this can help us better understand the meaning of the church-state debate today.

The New Testament commands Christians to respect the law and pray for worldly rulers. But in pagan Rome, there were some public duties believers could not and would not perform. Rulers who commanded obedience to just laws, peaceful conduct, or honesty in business dealings posed no moral problem for Christians. But burning incense to the *genius* (essence or spirit) of the emperor as a god—in effect, treating the state as divine—was a very different matter. Roman society made room for new gods quite willingly, as long as they made no exclusive claims. One emperor had a statue to Christ among the other gods in his home on the Palatine Hill. However, Christians believed in a new *kind* of god, and in Roman eyes, the Christian statement "Jesus is Lord!" had *political* content. The Christian God could not be content as the god of the local city, nor even of the great city itself, ancient Rome. In a way, Christians were martyred by the Romans for the same reason that Plato tells us Socrates was killed by the Greeks: *They did not worship the gods of the city.*[3] They obeyed just laws, but they referred everything to the ultimate source of every good, the one true God.

Roman anger at the new Christian cult as a form of sedition and impiety began early. It can be tracked from the writer Tacitus in the first century, through the persecution under Marcus Aurelius in the second century, to the last great persecution under Diocletian in the fourth century. From these bloody experiences, early Christians developed very mixed feelings about the state. Service in the military or as a public magistrate was often shunned. Origen, writing around AD 230, said that "Christians [should] decline public offices, not in order to escape these duties but in order to keep themselves for a more divine and necessary service in the church of God for the salvation of men."[4] He added, "We do not fight under [Caesar], although he require it; but we fight on his behalf . . . by offering our prayers to God."[5]

Hippolytus, around the same time, wrote that "a soldier of the government must be told not to execute men . . . He must be told not to take the military oath . . . A military governor or a magistrate of a city who wears the purple, either let him [resign] or let him be rejected. If a [candidate for baptism] or a baptized Christian wishes to become a soldier, let him be cast out, for he has despised God."[6] Tertullian also strongly discouraged Christian service in the military, and Tatian, as early as the middle of the second century, said, "[As a Christian,] I do not want to rule, I do not wish to be rich, I reject military command."[7]

All of this changed after Constantine. The revolutionary scope of his legacy reaches into the opening lines of *The Strategikon*, one of history's great texts on—ironically—waging war. Attributed to the emperor Maurice around AD 590, less than three centuries after Constantine's death, it begins:

> Let word and deed be guided by the All Holy Trinity, our God and Savior, the steadfast hope and assurance of divine assistance, who directs impor-

tant and beneficial undertakings to a favorable conclusion. Well aware of our own weakness, we have been motivated solely by a devotion to the nation. If then, what we have written should be deficient, the Holy Trinity will put it in order, turn it to our advantage and provide guidance for those who may read it. May this come about through the intercession of our Lady, the immaculate, ever-virgin Mother of God, Mary, and of all the saints; for blessed is our God for never ending ages of ages. Amen.[8]

In practice, Constantine's conversion led to a radically new mingling of the church and the political order. Earlier persecutions had kept the border between the two realms clear. But when Christianity became the official religion of the empire in AD 380 under the emperor Theodosius, the blending of the messy world of politics with the new faith revealed some ugly drawbacks. The "Christian emperor" Theodosius murdered seven thousand citizens of Thessalonica in 390. In response, Saint Ambrose, the great archbishop of Milan, banned him from entering churches until he did a harsh eight-month penance.

This shift in Christian status from a hated cult to the faith of the majority, including the imperial family, set a pattern for centuries. It led to a fusion of empire and church in the Byzantine East that flourished as a rich

Christian culture for more than one thousand years, until the Muslim seizure of Constantinople in 1453. The memory of Christian Rome continued in the barbarian West in the rise of the papacy; the role of the church as preserver of the past and mother of a new Europe; the medieval idea of sacred kingship; the Renaissance's divine right of kings; and the very notion of "Christendom." Remnants of the sacred nature of rule over men and women continue even today in the rituals of our own democratic system, including the use of a Bible in the oath of office. And even the liberation theology of the 1970s and 1980s, with its stress on *political* means to advance the kingdom of God, was a distant child of Constantine.

Modern critics of Constantine often claim, in the words of one Protestant writer, that "he muddled everything up by making conversion to Christianity financially and politically advantageous. He committed the sin of giving the church success. And so he is one of our worst embarrassments. He is the man secularists like to point to in order to warn everyone else what happens when Christians get their way."[9]

Critics argue that by tying herself too closely to the state, the church often lost her prophetic witness; that she went from persecuted to persecutor. They point to powerful cardinals like Richelieu and Mazarin in seventeenth-century France; the cynicism of Borgia and Medici popes in Renaissance Italy; and the brutality of Europe's Wars of Religion. Moreover—and this gets less attention—the state often got *more* than it gave away to the church through favorable concordats, the right to nominate and approve bishops, and pressure on papal elections.

The Protestant Reformation and Wars of Religion sharpened the tensions between religious and civil authority. They also raised new questions about the duties of believers. Even today, centuries later, the mental aftershocks of these "confessional" wars continue. In fact, the Enlightenment of the eighteenth century was, in a real sense, a reaction to their religious violence. Two of the deepest prejudices of Enlightenment thinkers were that religion is irrational and causes conflict between nations; and that church doctrine is a roadblock to human freedom. The desire for a totally secular state, both then and now, can often be tracked to these prejudices.

Voltaire summed up the French Enlightenment's contempt for Christianity—the church seen as a greedy, powerful peddler of superstition and cheerleader for public tyranny—when he urged *Écrasez l'infâme* (Crush the infamy). But curiously, and almost at the same moment as Voltaire, his fellow *philosophe* Jean-Jacques Rousseau accused Christianity of being too *other*worldly and, therefore, neglectful of its responsibilities for everyday human life. Furthermore, said Rousseau, the Christian faith divided nations over the competing claims of church and state, and split the very souls of believers: "Nobody ever quite succeeded in finding out just whom, as between ruler and priest, he was obliged to obey."[10] For the Enlightenment thinkers who despised her, the church had become too worldly and not worldly enough.

WRITING IN THE fifth century AD, less than one hundred years after Constantine, Saint Augustine of Hippo looked at the question of the Two Cities—the sacred and the worldly—in his masterwork, *The City of God*, which still influences Catholic political thought today. At a minimum, Augustine argued that the state should not hinder the free practice of the Christian faith. Preferably, the state should help advance the Gospel. But he believed that the more modest goal, what we might call a sound secularity, would usually be the case. Pope Gelasius I, following in this same tradition in AD 494, less than one hundred years after Saint Augustine, wrote in a letter to the emperor Anastasius in Constantinople:

> There are two powers, august emperor, by which this world is chiefly ruled, namely the sacred authority of the priests and the royal power. Of these, that of the priests is the more weighty, since they have to render an account for even the kings of men in the divine judgment. You are also aware, dear son, that while you are permitted honorably to rule over human kind, yet in things divine you bow your head humbly before the leaders of the

clergy and await from their hands the means of your salvation.[11]

This duality—the ultimate priority of religious matters, but the practical autonomy of civil authority and religious authority—became the Christian sense of church and state in the West for centuries. By the High Middle Ages, a scholar like Thomas Aquinas could speak of the two powers in an idiom that showed its affinities with both the ancient and modern West: "Human law is ordained for one kind of community, and the divine law for another kind, because human law is ordained for the civil community, implying mutual duties of man and his fellows . . . But the community for which the divine law is ordained is that of man in relation to God, either in this life or in the life to come."[12]

Aquinas did not entirely divide civil from divine law. In Aquinas, civil law has a moral function that should point us toward our perfection as rational beings; to the virtues we need in order to make good use of our minds and liberty in this world. Civil law that is simply an agreement arrived at by democratic procedure and guided by nothing higher than agreement can become gravely evil. In Germany, for example, Adolf Hitler came to power by legal, democratic means.

Still, even in his own day, Aquinas made a strong case for different sacred and civil functions. Just as no one wants a state dictating faith and morals, nobody wants a church claiming detailed expertise in public policy or economics. The Christian West, as nowhere else in the world, assigned political things to a space not shut off from God, but a space which had its own proper methods and demands.

The Catholic faith of our own modern era differs greatly from a belief system like Islam on questions involving religion and the state. But even our ancient and medieval Christian ancestors, though they would have said it differently, grasped that secular matters must be handled in a way distinct from sacred ones. At the same time, "secular space" does not imply or require secularism. Secularism is an ideology that seeks to exclude religious views from public life and marginalizes God himself. It is no more neutral toward religion than Marxism or fascism.

One insight American Catholics need to draw from these seventeen hundred years of wrestling with Constantine's legacy is best described as "limited government under God." Government is limited because politics by nature is limited, just as life in this world is limited. Politics does not exhaust our humanness. In fact, it's absent from the most important dimensions of life. Anyone who doubts this merely needs to think about his or her relationship with a child, spouse, or parent, a valued friend or colleague. We are much more than political animals.

Politics has nothing to say about much of our daily

experience, let alone our spiritual lives and walk with God. But even the proper secularity of limited government is *also* "under God" because the political realm must find, in its own imperfect manner, ways to bring about as much justice, peace, and order as circumstances allow. To do this, the secular depends on virtues that it cannot generate from within itself. In this sense, Christianity must stand above and in tension with democracy, while respecting the properly political. By forming people in virtues the world cannot, the church provides a vital public service, *especially* in a democracy.[13]

PAUL JOHNSON WROTE in his classic, *A History of Christianity*, that "it was the Christian spirit of mutual love and communal charity which most impressed pagans."[14] The social scientist Rodney Stark, author of *The Rise of Christianity*, draws the same conclusion.

Stark puts it this way: "The simple phrase, 'For God so loved the world . . .' would have puzzled an educated pagan. And the notion that the gods care how we treat one another would have been dismissed as patently absurd."[15] Stark argues that the Christian church conquered the Roman Empire *not* by celebrity conversion or opportunism or coercion, but mainly by the force of her beliefs and teaching.

Despite Constantine's huge political importance, Christianity had already grown so quickly *before* he came on the scene that Constantine's conversion was not just shrewd; it was probably inevitable. In other words, he didn't make the wave of history; he rode it. For Stark, "Christianity *did not* grow ... because Constantine said it should [emphasis in original]," but because Christians practiced what the church preached.[16] It was finally that simple. Christians lived their faith as the *most important* factor in their daily choices and actions. And that active witness of faith had revolutionary consequences.

As Stark writes, "An essential factor in the religion's success was what Christians believed . . . And it was the way those doctrines took on actual flesh, the way they directed organizational actions and individual behavior, that led to the rise of Christianity."[17] The most radical Christian belief, Stark says, was the belief in God's love and the commandment to love our neighbors as ourselves. Today, we often take these beliefs for granted. For some people, they're platitudes. But they marked something radically new in the history of religious witness.

America's founders understood that our political choices in the present flower out of the past; that a healthy republic requires a well-informed citizenry; and that part of being well informed means remembering and learning from history. So let me suggest what a few of the lessons for today's American Catholics might be.

First, the most powerful "political" act Catholics can

make is to love Jesus Christ, believe in his church, and *live her teachings*: not just in word but in all of their choices, decisions, and actions—public and private.

Second, despite the sins of Christians, the world still needs Jesus Christ. The record of modern unbelief—its wars, repressions, and genocides—is bloodier than anything in religious history. In fact, the Enlightenment's trust in the moral force of human reason "cleansed" of religion seems deader than Voltaire himself—who, we should note, despised Judaism even more than he did the Christian church. The nineteenth century's vanity, its naive overconfidence in progress, has become today's culture of doubt and cynicism—a space where not even human reason is safe from deconstruction, and not even the human person is seen as a unique kind of animal. As Christopher Dawson noted more than sixty years ago, "We can no longer [talk about] 'civilized men' for we are faced with the grim fact to which the Liberal optimism of [the nineteenth] century shut its eyes—the fact that a society can become inhuman while preserving all the technical and material advantages of an advanced scientific civilization."[18]

Third, as Christopher Lasch saw, the habit of unbelief, trickling down from the Enlightenment, runs strong in America's leadership classes, including the academy and media. And that has big consequences for the rest of us. Their distrust of religious faith, along with "[religion's] replacement by the remorselessly critical sensibility exemplified by psychoanalysis, and the degeneration of the 'analytical attitude' into an all out assault on ideals of every kind," has left American culture in a deeply wounded state.[19] Much of today's elite skepticism about religious faith assumes that religion is a kind of comfort food for the weak and dependent. But exactly the opposite is true.

Religious faith has *never* eliminated doubt about human meaning or suffering. Rather, as Lasch wrote, "Religious faith asserts the goodness of being in the face of suffering and evil. Black despair and alienation—which have their origin not in perceptions exclusively modern, but in the bitterness always felt toward a God who allows evil and suffering to flourish—often become the prelude to conversion."[20]

Jesus said the truth would make us free. He didn't say it would make us content or wipe away life's ambiguities. He also said, "Peace I leave with you, my peace I give to you; *not as the world gives* do I give to you [emphasis added]" (John 14:27). Christ didn't guarantee anything about worldly happiness. In fact, the Christian faith properly lived creates the habits of *self-criticism* and *concern for others*, and a hunger to act on both. Real faith is not an anesthetic. It's demanding, and it repudiates the main message of American consumer culture: that the world is all about *us*.

Fourth, the nature of the Gospel *forces* the church as a community and the individual Catholic as a believer to actively engage the world. That means all of it—including its social, economic, and political structures. We can argue about whether Constantine was inevitable. We can disagree about whether, in the long run, the church was more helped or hurt by his conversion and its results. But history is what it is; and we are all, in a sense, Constantine's children seventeen centuries removed, because the Gospel will *always* seek to penetrate and convert human affairs.

The Catholic Church has had many different relationships with many different states in many different eras. What we've learned is this: We will never build God's kingdom here on earth. When people have messianic expectations of the state, when they ask politics to deliver more than it can, the story ends badly.

But neither will we ever be released from the duty to sanctify, humanize, and bring Jesus Christ to the public square in which we live. And it is *precisely* because of this duty that the American experiment is so hopeful—and so important.

5.

THE AMERICAN EXPERIMENT

SOONER OR LATER, MOST American children learn the story of John Hancock. As president of the Second Continental Congress in 1776, he signed the Declaration of Independence larger than anyone else so that "King George III need not use his spectacles to read it." Even today, as the Declaration fades, Hancock's name stands out.

Members of the Congress signed the Declaration as a British army pursued George Washington's troops near New York City. Hancock and his colleagues, including Thomas Jefferson, John Adams, Benjamin Franklin, and others, gambled all they had for their new country. As the Declaration said, they risked "their lives, their fortunes and their sacred honor."

Hancock asked Maryland's Charles Carroll if he too would sign. Carroll was a lawyer and the Congress's only Catholic. He answered with the words "Most willingly." One colleague, suspicious of Carroll's Catholic faith, ap-

parently questioned his loyalty to the American cause. So
when Carroll signed his name, he added "of Carrollton,"
the name of his family's Maryland estate. In doing so,
Carroll made sure that the British Crown would have no
trouble tracking which "Charles Carroll" stood for independence. No other signer added a description to his
name.[1]

Carroll was born in Maryland in 1737. His parents
were of Irish Catholic descent. Sent to Catholic France at
age eight for his schooling, he later studied law in
Protestant London before returning to America in 1765.
Carroll knew Europe's religious divisions, the themes of
the Enlightenment, and the continent's growing intellectual ferment from firsthand experience.

In the year he arrived home, the British Parliament
passed taxes to help the empire pay for a recent war with
the French. For the first time, colonists were taxed directly from abroad, rather than by their own colonial leg-
islatures. Relations between the American colonies and
British Crown soured. As British abuses increased, Carroll became incensed. Along with young attorneys like
John Adams and Thomas Jefferson, he threw himself into
the revolutionary cause.

Unlike Adams and Jefferson, though, Carroll faced
an added danger. Not only did he risk treason against the
British Crown; he also broke Maryland law. By the laws
of his own colony, it was illegal for him—because he was
Catholic—to be politically active at all. In fact, under

Maryland law, Carroll could not earn a living as an attorney. He could not run for office. He could not even vote for others who *could* run for office—because his home colony, for whose freedom he was struggling, forbade it.

Then why did Carroll risk his life, family, and property? He had a simple answer. Carroll stepped forward "most willingly" because he wanted his freedom. That included his freedom to be Catholic. As he said years later: "To obtain religious as well as civil liberty, I entered zealously into the Revolution . . . God grant that this religious liberty may be preserved in these states, to the end of time, and that all who believe in the religion of Christ may practice the leading principle of charity, the basis of every virtue."[2]

Carroll later served in the U.S. Senate. He helped found the first U.S. diocese, now the Archdiocese of Baltimore. After Adams and Jefferson died in 1826, Carroll lived on as the only remaining signer of the Declaration. His life teaches a useful lesson. It embodies the American Catholic experience: a minority community barely tolerated and often harassed; but one that would loyally serve the nation.

FAR FROM THE Old World and its struggles, the Catholic Church in America would find a new model for the relations between church and state. But the "American experiment"—the idea that people of different faiths, cultures, and backgrounds might govern themselves by common principles—grew slowly. It did not emerge from theory. It came from hard experience. For in America, predominantly Protestant sects would need to learn something radically new: how to live together in peace.

A century before the birth of Charles Carroll, the first Puritan colonists settled at Plymouth Bay and later founded Massachusetts Bay Colony. From the start in America, Protestant Christianity was the native faith. Catholics were the immigrant newcomers. But even among Protestants, religious pluralism became a very painful challenge. The Puritans left an England where the Anglican Church still bore a Catholic imprint. These first American colonists wanted to purify the Christian faith of all traces of popery. That's a word we should remember: *purify*. The colonists did not want to escape religion. They wanted to do the opposite.

The Puritans sought to *cleanse* religion, to better witness their Christian beliefs. They wanted a pious society. Thus, they had little interest in tolerance. They simply wanted to avoid those religious ideas they disliked—and which they soon banned and expelled. The theologian Roger Williams, himself a Christian minister, founded Rhode Island Colony after Puritan leaders sent him into exile. Williams saw very clearly that agreement among the differing Christian sects of his day was unlikely. So Rhode Island formed a government committed to "liberty of conscience." Rather than settle religious disputes

with civil law, Williams argued that the Christian duty
was to learn to coexist.

A generation after settlers arrived at Plymouth,
Catholics fleeing England came to Maryland. They
founded St. Mary's City. At first, Maryland let Protes-
tants be Protestant, and Catholics be Catholic. Mary-
land's legislature passed a religious freedom bill in 1639.
In 1649, it approved an act guaranteeing religious rights.
But this tolerance did not last long. During the English
Civil Wars (1642–51), new Protestant colonists expelled
many of the Catholic settlers. They repealed both acts.
Later, in 1692, Anglicanism became the colony's religion. In 1704, Maryland passed "An Act to prevent the
Growth of Popery within this Province." It forbade the
Jesuits to, well, be Jesuits. Legislators did, however,
tweak the law so Catholics could worship privately.[3]

Maryland had the largest Catholic population in
America. But local Catholic numbers were still small.
They were even smaller in other colonies. One scholar to-
tals Catholics at thirty thousand on the eve of the Revolution, out of 3 million American colonists. Protestant
religious activity, on the other hand, was vigorous and
widespread. Even so, the thirteen colonies had no single,
dominant Christian church.

This pattern of strong but diverse Christian belief
led to practical accommodation. Virginia had made the
Anglican Church the official church of the common-
wealth. Yet it would soon tolerate "[even] Papists and

Quakers so long as they kept the peace." In 1744, Virginia changed its law requiring church attendance to allow "any Virginian to satisfy the law by attending the church of his choice." In 1759, the Reverend Andrew Burnaby did a religious survey of Philadelphia. To no one's surprise, he found a thriving array of "eight or ten places of religious worship; viz. two churches, three quaker meeting-houses, two Presbyterian ditto, one Lutheran church, one Dutch Calvinist ditto, one Swedish ditto, one Romish chapel, one Anabaptist meeting-house, one Moravian ditto, . . ."[4]

By the eve of the Revolution, American colonists, through luck, experience, and sheer need, had managed to do something unique. They had learned to live together in relative peace, despite their religious differences. Most colonies had an "established" church, but they also allowed other religious viewpoints. Maryland's discriminatory laws, which Charles Carroll knew so well, were generally not enforced.

DESPITE THE EASING of legal sanctions, anti-Catholic prejudice in the colonies remained harsh. The fact that colonial Catholics wanted more freedom to be Catholic does not fully explain Charles Carroll's trust in the Revolution. Revolutions, after all, can create worse regimes than they replace. But Carroll knew that he could sign the Declaration of Independence in good conscience because it had a strong, *natural law* content.

In its structure, the Declaration of Independence has a broad religious resonance. It refers several times to a Creator or Supreme Being. But more importantly, natural law principles shape the whole text. These principles have their roots in Christian medieval thought, which itself drew on the Hebrew tradition, classical Greek thought, and Roman jurists.

Natural law is not a sectarian idea. It is much larger and older than that. It exists in every society. Natural law teaches that all creation has a "nature," an inherent order and purpose. By using their reason, men and women can know what conforms to their human nature and is therefore good. This knowledge doesn't require a theology or law degree; we all instinctively sense it. Murder, lying, cheating, stealing, exploiting the poor, abusing the weak and elderly—these things are *universally* seen as evil whether a person is Jewish, Christian, Muslim, or agnostic, because they violate a natural law written into the human heart.

When Catholics oppose abortion, for example, they do so *not* because of some special Catholic religious doctrine or simply because the church says so. Rather, the church teaches abortion is wrong *because it already is.* Abortion violates the universal natural law by abusing the inherent human rights of the unborn child. The injustice of genocide, oppressing the poor, and killing unborn children is not a matter of religious doctrine. It's a matter of natural law.

Rooted in the natural law, the Declaration affirms that all nations are subject to a higher authority than their own man-made laws: "When in the Course of human events, it becomes necessary for one people to dissolve the political bands which have connected them with another, and to assume among the powers of the earth, *the separate and equal station to which the Laws of Nature and of Nature's God entitle them*, a decent respect to the opinions of mankind requires that they should declare the causes which impel them to the separation" (emphasis added).

Civil power answers to a higher authority. If a government ignores that higher authority, the governed have no duty to obey that civil power. Later in the Declaration, the signers argue that the British government has violated the colonists' natural rights to "life, liberty and the pursuit of happiness." In claiming their rights, the colonists were doing something historically unprecedented. Yet they were not claiming "new" rights, but their rights already *inherent in nature.*

The Declaration also saw human beings as "endowed by our Creator" with certain rights, and created equal—not equal in ability but equal in dignity as moral agents. In the mind of the founders, all human beings are both subject to the moral law and protected by it. These natural law concepts fitted smoothly with Charles Carroll's Catholic faith, even though they weren't explicitly Christian. The founders knew that freedom needs a virtuous people to survive. Lord Acton's famous phrase, harkening back as far as Saint Augustine, says it well: Freedom is "not the power of doing what we like, but the right of being able to do what we ought."

More than a decade later, in the wake of a successful American Revolution, the framers wrote a new Constitution. They sent it to the states for ratification. Critics of the Constitution had many complaints. Among them was the fact that it nowhere referred to God. The Constitution mentioned religion only once, stating that no religious test can be forced on any citizen seeking public office. But again, this fitted very well with Catholic natural law tradition. For the framers, the new federal government had no authority in theological matters. It should not therefore judge the religious fitness of any person seeking public office.

Critics also worried that the Constitution had no bill of rights. Religious freedom had no *explicit* guarantee. James Madison, a strong supporter of religious freedom and the Father of the Constitution, said such guarantees were unneeded. He thought that all religious communities were already protected under the new federal government. Madison argued that the nation's Christian sects, by their sheer number, would block any sects from ever uniting to threaten another group. He also feared that including a bill of rights might limit freedom. He reasoned that if such a bill were added, and some rights were not listed, then those rights would implicitly *not* be protected.[5]

The critics proved more persuasive. And in light of recent history, we can be grateful that a bill of rights won out. The Constitution's First Amendment ensures the free exercise of religion. We're fortunate to have it. Madison, despite his genius, might have a very hard time making sense of today's hostility to religion in public discourse. So might George Washington. As Washington said in his Farewell Address, "Of all the dispositions and habits which lead to political prosperity, religion and morality are indispensable supports." He went on to warn against the mistaken idea "that morality can be maintained without religion."

Madison might be even more baffled by today's debates over separation of church and state. Virtually all Americans accept the principle of keeping religious and civil authority separate. But what that principle means is less clear. The First Amendment's religion clause merely states that "Congress shall make no law respecting an establishment of religion, or prohibiting the free exercise thereof." Scholars differ sharply on what the clause really mandates. For "strict separationists," it means that government should be religion-neutral, even to the point of state hostility to any official public recognition of religion. For "nonpreferentialists," it means that government is free to acknowledge and even support religion, so long as no single religious group gets preferred treatment.

But neither argument would have had much relevance for the framers. In the actual circumstances, a key reason the First Amendment barred any official federal religion was that various states *already had* tax-supported established churches and wanted to keep them. Few saw this as violating religious freedom or the integrity of civil power. In fact, some states continued to officially support their churches for decades after the Constitution took effect.

The one thing the "establishment clause" *cannot* mean—either from the Constitution's wording and core principles or from the intent of the framers—is for religious believers and communities to be silent in public affairs.

WHEN CHARLES CARROLL chose to support the American rebellion, it was uncertain what the outcome would be, even if the Revolution succeeded. Some of the founders, notably New York's John Jay, did not wish to extend religious freedom to Catholics. Quebec Catholics refused to join the rebels because they feared that a colonial victory would end the religious tolerance they already enjoyed from the British Crown. On the other side, Loyalists (Tories) warned that the Revolution's alliance with France might lead to the French imposing the Catholic faith in America.

But the founders soon showed that they took religious liberty seriously. During the Constitutional Convention of 1787, members made a point of attending services in the various churches of Philadelphia, including the Catholic chapel. The visit was distasteful for some, but religious liberty meant precisely that personal prejudices should be overcome, with everyone treated equally under the law.

What that implied in practice became clear at an early stage. In the 1780s, when establishing an American Catholic hierarchy, the Holy See asked the American government its thoughts about the impending matter—and was astounded to receive the reply that the government had no view. Never before had *any* government conceded to the church full liberty of self-government.

Thus free of government meddling, Catholics in the United States found an ideal space to thrive. This applied both to Catholics as individuals and to the church as a public, believing community. American Catholics had no problem with the lack of an established church. In fact, because of it, their own freedom was more secure. And this security offered very favorable conditions for Catholics, as a European observer, Alexis de Tocqueville, soon noted.

Arriving in America in 1831, Tocqueville was struck

by the "religious atmosphere of the country." Tocqueville, a French Catholic, came from a nation that had suffered a far bloodier and bitterly anticlerical revolution a decade after the American Revolution. He published two volumes of his classic, *Democracy in America.* About 1 million Catholics lived in America by the time he traveled the country. He noticed that "these Catholics are very loyal in the practice of their worship and full of zeal and ardor for their beliefs. Nevertheless, they form the most republican and democratic of all classes in the United States."

Tocqueville saw that, contrary to Protestant fears of the day, the Catholic faith did not oppose American democracy, but instead strengthened it. He wrote:

> In matters of dogma, the Catholic faith places all intellects on the same level; the learned man and the ignorant, the genius and the common herd, must all subscribe to the same details of belief; rich and poor must follow the same observances, and it imposes the same austerities upon the strong and the weak; it makes no compromise with any mortal, but applying the same standard to every human being, it mingles all classes of society at the foot of the same altar, just as they are mingled in the sight of God . . . Thus, American Catholics are both the most obedient of the faithful and the most independent citizens.

Tocqueville was struck by America's vivid Christian atmosphere; but also by the intense religious *activity*: "America is still the place where the Christian religion has kept the greatest real power over men's souls; and nothing better demonstrates how useful and natural it is to man, since the country where it now has widest sway is both the most enlightened and the freest." This was very different from what he had seen in Europe, where he had watched

> the spirits of religion and of freedom almost always marching in opposite directions. In America, I found them intimately linked together in joint reign over the same land. I found that they all agreed with each other except about details; all thought that the main reason for the quiet sway of religion over their country was the complete separation of church and state. I have no hesitation in stating that throughout my stay in America I met nobody, law or cleric, who did not agree about that.

In America, people understood that to be free themselves, their churches must be free; but those same churches must also be active in shaping virtuous citizens. Admitting that he spent more time with Catholic priests than Protestant ministers, Tocqueville said:

I have known Americans to form associations to send priests out into the new states of the West and establish schools and churches there; they fear that religion might be lost in the depths of the forest and that the people growing up there might be less fitted for freedom . . . How could society escape destruction if, when political ties are relaxed, moral ties are not tightened? And what can be done with a people master of itself if it is not subject to God?[6]

Tocqueville's optimism about America was well grounded. The freedom and opportunities of the new nation drew millions of immigrants. Many were Catholic. By the nation's first centenary in 1876, the Catholic Church had become America's largest single Christian community. Anti-Catholic prejudice—fruitless, but bitter and ugly—also grew. Bigotry took the form of economic and political discrimination against Catholics, scandal-mongering, legal bullying of Catholic schools, orphanages, and other institutions, and even violence.

But as new waves of immigrants arrived, tensions over the relationship between church and American society also grew within the church herself. By the 1890s, American bishops had divided roughly between two camps, the Americanists, led by Archbishop John Ireland of St. Paul, and more traditional bishops, led by Archbishop Michael Corrigan of New York. The Americanists argued that, despite widespread anti-Catholic prejudice, conditions in the United States were remarkably open to the Catholic Church. Catholics could therefore confidently embrace American democratic ideas. Conservatives were more wary of modern political thought. They also feared the consequences of assimilation.

Pope Leo XIII sided against the Americanists with his 1895 encyclical *Longinqua Oceani*. His key thought was this:

> For the Church amongst you, unopposed by the Constitution and government of your nation, fettered by no hostile legislation, protected against violence by the common laws and impartiality of the tribunals, is free to live and act without hindrance. Yet, though all this is true, it would be very erroneous to draw the conclusion that in America is to be sought the type of the most desirable status of the Church, or that it would be universally lawful or expedient for State and Church to be, as America, dissevered and divorced.[7]

We can better understand Leo XIII's words if we consider their context. He lived at a time when the church in Europe faced bitter and sometimes violent pressure from revolutionary movements and anticlerical governments. Politically, economically, and scientifically, the world was rapidly changing. Much of the change seemed hostile. Some of it clearly *was* hostile. Nothing in the emerging new age seemed to guarantee the church's safety, as Europe's former Christian social order once had.

Leo XIII could not see the future. Events would prove Archbishop Ireland right in important ways. Catholics would thrive in a free American republic grounded in the rule of law and ordered liberty. Unfortunately, history would also show that assimilation has a cost.

EXACTLY TWO HUNDRED years after Charles Carroll returned to America from Europe in 1765, the work of another American Catholic, John Courtney Murray, bore fruit in Rome. The last session of the Second Vatican Council (1962–65) debated a statement on religious liberty shaped in important ways by Murray's Catholic experience of American democracy.

Born in 1904, Murray later entered the Jesuits and studied at Boston College. He was ordained a priest in 1933, the year Hitler came to power in Germany. He earned his doctorate from Rome's Pontifical Gregorian University in 1937, specializing in dogmatic theology. His time in a bitterly divided Europe left a deep impression. Murray was stunned by the continent's rapid falling away from Christianity; by the aggressive unbelief he saw not only in brutal systems like national socialism and communism, but throughout European life. He watched firsthand as societies without God relentlessly produced a dehumanized public life.

Murray also saw that because of its prosperity, its religious founding, its different political heritage (through the Scottish rather than the French Enlightenment), and the lack of religious warfare in its past, America was different. In practice, American freedom meant freedom *for* belief. Continental freedom implied freedom *from* religion. Murray grasped that Leo XIII's fears about separating church and state were not, at their root, a reactionary defense of church privilege.[8] Rather, they derived from Leo's very real struggle against European laicism—a belligerent, antireligious secularism that swallowed all opposition by identifying society and the public good exclusively with the state.

In his classic, *We Hold These Truths: Catholic Reflections on the American Proposition* (1960), Murray argued that the Catholic faith and American democracy are not merely compatible but congenial. Unlike continental revolutions, the American Revolution had created a civil government with strictly limited powers; a government *subordinate* to society; a government that claimed no competence in religious matters and did not seek to separate religion from society, but only from the order of law. Like Charles Carroll before him, Father Murray saw that the Declaration of Independence, rooted in the natural law, held that "the life of man in society under government is founded on truths, on a certain body of objective truth, universal in its import, accessible to the reason of man."[9]

For Murray, the First Amendment created room for American Catholics to thrive. He saw that by confirming religious authority and civil authority as distinct, the First Amendment served religious communities as well as it did the state. Catholics could look to Europe, with its legacy of incestuous links between religion and the state, to see that the church was usually the loser in such bargains. In America, the church had independence. She controlled her own spiritual order. These conditions encouraged Catholics to fully—and "most willingly"—contribute to American life.

Murray argued that religion, especially the Christian faith, provides "ultimate or transcendent meaning" to a nation's public life. He believed in American democratic principles because "religious pluralism is theologically the human condition." He called for cooperative dialogue among Protestants, Catholics, Jews, and secularists, using the natural law as a common language through which to build the common good. Murray hoped Catholics would play a leading role in that conversation because of their natural law tradition.

Murray rejected the model of Catholic "confessional states," dominant in the Catholic world since the Reformation. Instead, he pressed a model of liberty rooted in the American experience but harkening back to earlier Christian thought and a more authentic Christian tradition. Like Pope Gelasius I many centuries before him, Murray believed in the ultimate priority of religious matters. But also like Gelasius, he saw that a mutually respectful autonomy of secular authority and sacred authority can coexist.

Rome in the 1940s and 1950s did not share his views. For arguing the American model of religious freedom so vigorously, Murray's superiors in Rome "suggested" that he cease writing on the subject. Murray obediently complied. He was not invited to the opening session of the Second Vatican Council. But Murray's views coincided with those of a great many American bishops, who were determined to see religious freedom affirmed. A New York cardinal named Francis Spellman, who was no theologian, knew that Murray was the best intellectual resource the Americans had.

Spellman brought Murray along as an adviser to Vatican II's second session. It was a wise choice. Murray played a key role in drafting the third and fourth versions of a decisive statement by the council on religious freedom. And on the content of the Second Vatican Council—on what it said, and on what it *didn't* say—American Catholic life has turned ever since.

6.

A NEW DISPENSATION

IN 1084, A YEAR before his death in exile, an anguished Pope Saint Gregory VII wrote, "I cry, I cry and I cry again . . . The religion of Christ, the true faith, has fallen so low that it is an object of scorn not only to the devil but to Jews and Saracens and pagans . . . These keep their law, as they believe it; but we, intoxicated with the world, have deserted our law."[1]

We can take two lessons from his words. The first is this: All people are shaped by their time. Gregory wrote in an age of fierce princely intrigue and strong anti-Judaism. He also wrote just a decade before the First Crusade, and three decades after the Great Schism with Eastern Christianity. In other words, he faced a fractured Christian world under siege from four hundred years of Muslim jihad.

The second lesson is this: Despite the sins we find in every church generation, renewal always reasserts itself. Gregory VII was one of the great reformers in Catholic history. He weakened the power of the state over church affairs. He attacked the practice of selling church offices. He fought to purify a corrupt clergy. He worked to restore zeal for Jesus Christ among the faithful. Later centuries saw uglier behavior from some church leaders: a scandalous papacy, the abuse of church power, and the stagnation that led to the Reformation. But in a way, that proves a point. The hunger for Christian renewal throughout history is a sign of life in response to a peculiar illness. Among believers, the sickness takes different forms in different ages, but the illness is always the same.

Cardinal John Henry Newman identified the problem eight hundred years after Gregory VII. He said that the conduct of most Christians was barely different from what it would have been otherwise, "neither much better nor much worse, if they believed Christianity to be a fable." In other words, they lacked real faith.[2]

LESS THAN A year after the Second Vatican Council closed, a young scholar published his memories of the great gathering. He had attended the council as a *peritus*, or theological expert. He had helped in drafting the texts. He had heard the debates firsthand. And looking back in 1966, he wrote the following words:

> The debate on religious liberty will in later years be considered one of [Vatican II's] most important

events . . . there was in St. Peter's the sense that here was the end of the Middle Ages, the end even of the Constantinian age. Few things had hurt the Church so much in the last 150 years as its tenacious clinging to outmoded politico-religious positions. The attempt to use the state as a protector of faith from the threat of modern science served more than anything else to undermine the faith and prevent the needed spiritual regeneration. It supported the idea of the Church as an enemy of freedom, as a Church which feared science and progress—products of human intellectual freedom—and thereby became one of the most powerful causes of anti-clericalism. We need not add that, here too, the evil dates far back. The use of the state by the Church for its own purposes, climaxing in the Middle Ages and in absolutist Spain in the early modern era, has, since Constantine, been one of the most serious liabilities of the Church, and any historically minded person is inescapably aware of this.

He added:

In its thinking, the Church has stubbornly confused faith in the absolute truth manifest in Christ with an insistence on an absolute secular status for the institutional Church. Another characteristic deeply embedded in the Catholic mentality is the inability to see beyond the Catholic faith, the inability to see the other person's viewpoint . . . Yet such habits have characterized Church teaching on the relations of Church and state right up to [the Second Vatican Council].[3]

In the same text, the author caught the drama of the council's great themes. He asked, "Was the intellectual position of 'anti-Modernism'—the old policy of exclusiveness, condemnation and defense leading to an almost neurotic denial of all that was new—to be continued? Or would the Church, after it had taken all the necessary precautions to protect the faith, turn over a new leaf and move on into a new and positive encounter" with its own origins and the world of today?[4]

The young German priest who wrote those words was Joseph Ratzinger. In speaking so bluntly about the value of religious liberty, Ratzinger linked himself to one of the key concerns of American Catholics. He set himself against a flawed way of thinking about Catholic engagement with the world. He aligned himself with a new moment in the church, a "new dispensation" for Christian action. But we can only grasp what that really meant, and means now, by recalling the council itself.

History has seen twenty-one ecumenical councils. To be authentic, a council must be convened or at least accepted by the bishop of Rome. The word *ecumenical* comes from the Greek *oikoumene,* or "world." All ecumenical councils involve bishops and other invited participants from around the globe. Each of these gatherings has helped shape the church. Some, like Nicaea and Trent, have been decisive. Some have been turbulent. Most have dealt with a problem or crisis. But Vatican II, coming less than a century after the troubled First Vatican Council, happened at a time of seeming vigor in the Catholic world. It took most people by surprise. It faced no urgent doctrinal dispute. It offered no new dogmas. Yet for all those who experienced the council and its aftermath as Catholic adults, it was transforming. Decades later, Vatican II remains one of the central events of their lives.

Authors have written many books about the council. We don't need to repeat their work here. But we do need to understand that when Pope Pius XII died in the autumn of 1958, both the world and the church had reached a tipping point—a moment when apparently unrelated factors could combine to create rapid change.

The decade between 1945 and 1955 saw the end of the Second World War; the Marshall Plan; the Nuremberg trials; public revelations of the Holocaust; the end of colonialism; the founding of the United Nations; the founding of the State of Israel; the First Arab-Israeli War; the First India-Pakistan War; the Greek Civil War; the Iron Curtain; the Cold War; the Chinese Civil War; the First Indochina War; the beginning of the Second Indochina War; the Korean War; jet travel; the first computers; the Salk polio vaccine; fission and fusion nuclear bombs; the arms race; television; and a little device very few people understood at the time: the transistor.

A single technological change—the Gutenberg printing press—reshaped the entire culture of Europe in the fifteenth and sixteenth centuries. Martin Luther used the printed word with revolutionary effect, and in practice, technology is never neutral. A major new technology does not "add" to a culture. It reorganizes it. As one modern scholar observed, "New technologies alter the structure of our interests: the things we think *about*. They alter the character of our symbols: the things we think *with*. And they alter the nature of community: the arena in which thoughts develop."[5] In the years leading up to Vatican II, *dozens* of such changes took place. The results were deep and unpredictable. They touched not just the external conditions of life but also its inner balance. And for the first time in history, the impact was global because of vastly improved communications. The poor of the developing world could *know* they were poor, and what that meant, because they could know, in real time, how the developed world lived.

The last years of Pius XII hid the ferment brewing even within the church. A bishop friend of mine once told me that every pope and every bishop is part "museum curator." And it's quite true. The past makes the foundation for the present. Catholics have a duty to protect it. They can't forget or rewrite their history without undermining who they are. But reverence for the past can also become a pious habit of inertia; a dislike of change or new thought. The church in 1958 had been shaped by four hundred years of confessional conflict with Protestants. Compounding that were two hundred years of sometimes bloody belligerence from European secular elites. Compounding that was a knowledge revolution. Compounding that were deep social and economic changes. And compounding *that* was the challenge of the great atheist systems of the early twentieth century.

The Catholic response was embodied in the reactive toughness of Pius IX in the late nineteenth century. That was followed by Pius X's antimodernism in the decree *Lamentabili Sane* and in his encyclical *Pascendi Dominici Gregis* in the early twentieth. These actions, however understandable in context, marked Catholic intellectual life for a generation. As then Father (later Cardinal) Avery Dulles wrote in 1977, the more radical Catholic reformers of the early twentieth century—the modernists—believed that Christianity had "an indefinite capacity to adapt itself to the trends of the times," no matter how troubling.

"In the face of this threat, Rome felt compelled to react in what can only be called a heavy-handed manner. Failing to give recognition to what was legitimate in the Modernist program," Dulles noted, Rome fell back on authoritarianism.[6] Thus, Catholic life in the 1950s ap-

peared solid, but the church also suffered from brittle-
ness. More and more people felt a need for renewing the
Catholic faith in a way true to its Christ-given mission.

Pius XII's successor, Cardinal Angelo Roncalli (Pope
John XXIII), offered a striking contrast to the man he
followed. Pius XII came from an established, aristocratic
family. John XXIII, elected in October 1958 at the age
of seventy-seven, came from Italian peasant stock. In the
place of papal formality, John XXIII radiated warmth.
He could also command, as he did in April 1959 when
he forbade Catholics to vote for parties supporting communism. And he was nobody's fool, as his own Curia
soon learned. Much of the Catholic world assumed that
John XXIII would serve as a caretaker on the road to a
younger pope. But less than three months after his election, in January 1959, he announced the convening of a
new ecumenical council. He lived to open Vatican II in
1962. He did not live to close it, dying in 1963 just two
months after releasing his encyclical *Pacem in Terris*
(Peace on Earth). But in the brief five years he served as
bishop of Rome, John XXIII returned the papal ministry
from medieval princeling to good shepherd; from castle
lord to the real meaning of *pontifex*—that is, "bridge
builder."

We can't understand Vatican II without grasping the
spirit of the pope who called it. John XXIII was a man of
unusual pastoral skill. He was alert to the concerns of
others. He had a strong sense of social justice. He saw the

evil of the arms race. He respected the achievements of the modern world. He was also a globalist. He understood the suffering of people in the developing countries; the priority of the poor; and the mission of the Catholic faith to all persons, in all cultures, in all ages. And yet he sifted all these concerns through a heart shaped by his episcopal motto: "obedience and peace." John XXIII never saw the church as a problem that needed fixing, or a corporation at civil war with its soul. The Catholic Church was one reality, an intimately personal unity summed up in his great encyclical *Mater et Magistra*, issued a year before the council: "Mother and Teacher of all nations—such is the Catholic Church in the mind of her Founder, Jesus Christ; to hold the world in an embrace of love, that men, in every age, should find in her their own completeness in a higher order of living, and their ultimate salvation. She is 'the pillar and ground of the truth.' "[7]

Charles de Foucauld once wrote that obedience is the yardstick of love. For John XXIII, any love of the church that claimed to express itself as *disobedience* to her teaching would have been impossible to imagine.

IN OPENING THE council on October 11, 1962, the pope gave his reasons for convening it. He said that he wanted "to assert once again the Magisterium [teaching authority of the church], which is unfailing and perdures until the end of time, in order that this Magisterium, taking into account the errors, the requirements and the opportunities of our time, might be presented in exceptional form to all men throughout the world."[8]

He named the council's greatest concern as this: "that the sacred deposit of Christian doctrine should be guarded and taught more efficaciously." He tasked the attending bishops with "[transmitting] the doctrine, pure and integral, without any attenuation or distortion, which through 20 centuries . . . has become the common patrimony of men." At the same time, he disagreed "with those prophets of gloom who are always forecasting disaster." He said the church "must ever look to the present, to the new conditions and new forms of life introduced into the modern world which have opened new avenues to the Catholic apostolate." He said that the substance of the Catholic faith is one thing, but the way it is presented is another. And crucially, he urged the attending bishops to treat the errors of the modern world with "the medicine of mercy rather than that of severity" and by "demonstrating the validity of [church] teaching rather than by condemnations." With those words, and without weakening in any way the continuity of Catholic teaching, John XXIII set the council on a very different course from the previous century.

Encouraged by the pope, two principles came to guide council life. The first was *aggiornamento*, an Italian word that means "bringing up to date." Catholics see salvation history as a continuing, organic story. The past was made by human beings shaped by the good and evil, the knowledge and ignorance, of their specific time. Renewal in the church always seeks to correct past sins, but it never repudiates history. Thus, the council did not seek to remake the church from the ground up. It did not seek to change her basic mission or doctrines. It did not seek to weaken the vocation of the Catholic Church as "mother and teacher" of all humanity. Instead, the council sought to make the church *more* fruitful in her work by reinvigorating the forms and means of Catholic life in the light of new conditions. *Aggiornamento* called for a fresh way of thinking. It required the church to listen to the times. It invited a new openness to—and new engagement with—the world.

The second principle guiding the council was *ressourcement,* a French word meaning "return to the sources." It gave a framework to *aggiornamento.* The council knew that a pristine ancient Christianity never really existed. The Gospel has always been lived by real people in real circumstances, with all the human sins, virtues, and conflicts that real life involves. Reinventing the Christian faith has never worked. Resetting the Catholic clock to some pure but imaginary Christian moment in the past has likewise always failed. Every attempt to do so has been, in practice, a subtle lack of faith in Christ himself, who promised to be with the church always. The structures and habits of Catholic life, which arose over the centuries, sometimes became an obstacle to faith. But just as often, they nourished the faith and guarded it from changing its nature along with changing social environments. History is a record of the encounter between character and circumstance. The present can't elude the past. Every age builds on both the good and the bad from the generations that preceded it.

Thus, the council sought to renew Catholic life by revisiting the ancient sources of Christian belief for answers to the questions posed by modern life. Yves Congar, a Dominican theological expert at the council, said that "only a profound understanding of the tradition can guide [the church] to discern the useful elements in modernity, to select them with certainty, to adapt them with tact."[9] Henri de Lubac, a Jesuit *peritus* at the council, stressed that

> in the last analysis, what is needed is not a Christianity that is more virile, or more efficacious, or more heroic, or stronger; it is that we should live our Christianity with more virility, more efficacy, more strength, and if necessary, more heroism— but we must live it as it is. There is nothing that should be changed in it, nothing that should be corrected, nothing that should be added (which does not mean however, that there is not a continual need to keep its channels from silting up); it is not a case of adapting it to the fashion of the day.

[The Christian faith] must come into its own again
in our souls. We must give our souls back to it.[10]

The bishops saw that real renewal could not just condemn modern evil. Neither could it bring back the past.
Neither could it change the basic mission and identity of
the church. As the council said later in its own documents, "Every renewal of the Church essentially consists
in an increase of fidelity to her own calling."[11] In fact, the
council never intended, and never did anything to suggest, that the church should abandon her mandate to
"make disciples of all nations" (Matthew 28:19).

Thus the council would seek to offer the Catholic
faith more compellingly to the modern heart. It wanted
to call Catholics more deeply to prayer and then to action; and to make the church better at her mission of
bringing the world to Jesus Christ, and Jesus Christ to
the world. To do this, said Avery Dulles, Vatican II had
two key points of focus: the interior renewal of Catholic
life, and the building of stronger bonds "between the
Church and other human communities—the other Christian Churches, the other religions and the secular culture
of our age." These two goals were linked. The bishops
hoped that a more open approach to the world "would
greatly assist the Catholic Church in its own self-
renewal, and that that renewal, in turn, would enable the
Church to relate itself more effectively to the rest of the
human family."[12]

Doing that turned out to be harder than imagined. Catholics believe that God guides the church in an intimate way. But he works through human beings. As a result, every ecumenical council involves a struggle of ideas. Vatican II was no exception. The council needed three years of preparation. And a Roman curial staff shaped mentally by the conflictive first half of the twentieth century did much of that work—some seventy turgid "schemata" for discussion, totaling more than two thousand pages.

As a young Joseph Ratzinger wrote in 1966, "How were the [council's bishops] to wade through this verbal wilderness? How was the council to distill from all this material a message meaningful" to modern man? Wasn't it much more likely "that the council would ultimately issue a fearsome kind of dogmatic supercompendium which would weigh down upon any future work like a heavy millstone?"[13] Along with the problem of a huge and preprogrammed agenda was another fact. Most of the 2,500 attending bishops and other participants didn't know each other. As Ratzinger noted, "Although there were strong, unifying bonds between the individual bishops and Rome, there were hardly any 'horizontal' ties among the bishops themselves. These really should have constituted an essential element of Catholicity." Yet most of the bishops had never worked together, even when they came from the same country.[14]

Between October 1962 and December 1965, Vatican II met in four sessions. Despite early obstacles, the council produced four major constitutions and twelve decrees and declarations. These touched on nearly every vital aspect of Catholic life, from the reform of the Liturgy, the nature of divine revelation, and the identity of the church; to the role of bishops, the ministry of priests, Christian education, and the dignity of the layperson. Disagreements occurred on all these issues. Sometimes the discussions were heated. But given the gravity of the material involved, motives were rarely as simpleminded as some reporters suggested. In fact, no ecumenical council can be understood mainly through a sociological or political lens without destroying its real meaning. Every council is more than the sum of its actors, factions, and issues. It must be judged by its words and results, in the light of faith.

The debates over religious liberty; the church and non-Christian religions, and the Catholic approach to the modern world were among the council's hardest work. But given Vatican II's pastoral theme, with the practical results it implied, these debates also ranked among the most crucial. They finished only in the council's final days. But they were very far-reaching. They still shape American Catholic life today.

. . .

A HAPPILY MARRIED friend of mine once said that talking about what the Second Vatican Council could have said, or should have said, or almost did, or might have done, is like talking about the woman he almost married before he met his wife. "Life would have been very different," he said, "except it isn't." The teaching of Vatican II exists first and foremost in the council documents themselves. No interpretation of the council has merit unless it proceeds organically from *what the council actually said*, and then remains true to it.[15]

The work of the council's final session in 1965 rooted itself in the church's self-understanding. That identity had found renewed expression in the great Dogmatic Constitution on the Church (*Lumen Gentium*) at the end of the third session in November 1964. *Lumen Gentium* reaffirmed Catholic belief in the "necessity of faith and baptism"; that "the Church, a pilgrim now on earth, is necessary for salvation"; that "all men are called to belong to the new People of God" embodied in the Catholic Church; and that no one could be saved "who, knowing the Catholic Church was founded as necessary by God through Christ, would refuse either to enter it or remain in it" (LG 13–14).

It also taught that "[Christ's] Church, constituted and organized as a society in the present world, subsists in the Catholic Church, which is governed by the successor of Peter and the bishops in communion with him."

But at the same time, it said, "Nevertheless, many elements of sanctification and of truth are found outside its visible confines." It stressed that non-Catholics and non-Christians "who nevertheless seek God with a sincere heart" and try in their actions to "do His will as they know it through the dictates of their conscience—these too may achieve eternal salvation." And the same hope applied to those nonbelievers "who, without any fault of theirs, have not yet arrived at an explicit knowledge of God and who, not without grace, strive to lead a good life" (LG 8, 16).

In other words, *Lumen Gentium* both affirmed and adjusted Catholics' understanding of their church. It confirmed papal authority but restored the collegiality of bishops. It confirmed the hierarchical nature of the church but restored the Catholic sense of *communio*—that is, the church as a communion of free persons and local churches. It confirmed the unique priesthood of the ordained but restored an awareness of the common priesthood of all believers and the dignity of laypersons, each of whom shares "in the obligation of spreading the faith to the best of his ability" (LG 17).

The thought behind *Lumen Gentium* shaped the council's last session. Three documents, finished in Vatican II's final weeks, framed the modern Catholic approach to pluralistic society and the public square: the Declaration on the Relation of the Church to Non-

Christian Religions (*Nostra Aetate*), the Declaration on Religious Liberty (*Dignitatis Humanae*), and the Pastoral Constitution on the Church in the Modern World (*Gaudium et Spes*).

The world knows *Nostra Aetate* (In this age of ours) mainly for its reflection on the Jewish people. *Nostra Aetate* rejected any claim of collective Jewish responsibility for the death of Jesus. It rejected "all hatreds, persecution, displays of anti-Semitism leveled at any time or from any source against the Jews" (NA 4). Whether anyone drafting this text sensed how pivotal it would be is unclear. *Nostra Aetate* has about sixteen hundred words. Barely six hundred deal with the Jewish people. But it led to a sea change in Catholic-Jewish relations. It also led to a deeper understanding by Catholics of their own religious identity and origins in Judaism.

And even this was only part of *Nostra Aetate*'s significance. The declaration affirmed the sanctity of all persons as created in the image of the same God. It stressed that Catholics should reject "nothing that is true and holy" in other religions (NA 2). It reproved, "as foreign to the mind of Christ, any discrimination against people or any harassment of them on the basis of their race, color, condition in life or religion" (NA 5).

Dignitatis Humanae (Of human dignity) reframed the relationship of religious truth to religious freedom. Influenced by the thought of John Courtney Murray and the American Catholic experience, the declaration stressed each person's right to freedom from coercion in religious matters. It acknowledged that through conscience, man recognizes the demands of the divine law. Therefore, he is "bound to follow this conscience faithfully." He must not be forced "to act contrary to his conscience. Nor must he be prevented from acting according to his conscience, especially in religious matters" (DH 3). *Dignitatis Humanae* argued, in effect, that while error may have no rights, human beings do. All persons have a God-given right to believe as their conscience demands. Truth can only be *proposed.* It cannot be *imposed* without violating the sanctity of the individual person and subverting the truth itself.

Finally, in *Gaudium et Spes* (Joy and hope) the council offered solidarity with the whole human family. It said the church can and must learn from the good things in the modern world. Catholics should work with all persons of goodwill to build mutual understanding and a just society. The secular order has its own true autonomy, for "the political community and the Church are autonomous and independent of each other in their own fields." *Gaudium et Spes* stressed that the church should never place its hopes "in any privileges accorded to it by civil authority; indeed it will give up the exercise of certain legitimate rights whenever it becomes clear that their use will compromise the sincerity of its witness, or whenever new circumstances call for a revised approach" (GS 76). In other words, Vatican II closed with an extraordinary statement of trust in humanity's ability to seek the truth—and humanity's willingness to live it.

"I THINK IT is important to note," Joseph Ratzinger wrote in 1966, that

> with all our satisfaction over the work of the council's renewal, we not overlook certain ingredients of injustice, those little touches of Pharisaism which all too readily accompany this joy. Very much indeed did the Church need renewal from within in the new situation of today. Yet it must not be forgotten that the Church has always remained the Church, and that at any time in history, the way of the Gospel could be found and was found in it . . . The faith of those who are simple of heart is the most precious treasure of the Church. *To serve and to live this faith is the noblest vocation in the renewal of the Church.* [emphasis added][16]

Henri de Lubac and Yves Congar had both obediently suffered criticism from Roman authorities in the years before Vatican II. But that obedience, the yardstick of their love, proved fruitful. The impact of their own and other similar thinking on the council was immense. In fact, the council owed almost everything it achieved to the Catholic biblical, liturgical, and patristic renewal movements in the decades preceding it. In later years, Pope John Paul II—himself an active young bishop at Vatican II—named both de Lubac and Congar to the College of Cardinals. Joseph Ratzinger later directed the Congregation for the Doctrine of the Faith. In 2005, forty years after the council closed, he was elected Pope Benedict XVI.

John XXIII wanted the council to be "pastoral" in the original sense. A pastor is a shepherd and guide. The word comes from the Latin verb *pascere,* which means "to feed." In John's mind, the council should neither indulge nor condemn the modern world. Rather, the church should seek even more zealously to lead all people—through goodwill and a frank dialogue motivated by love—to their destiny in God. In his opening comments to the council, he voiced the hope that "by bringing herself up to date where required . . . the Church will make men, families and people really turn their minds *to heavenly things*" (emphasis added). He reminded the Catholic world that "our mortal life is to be ordered in such a way as to fulfill our duties as citizens of earth and of heaven," and that we should seek first the kingdom of God and his justice (Matthew 6:33).

Like Gregory VII nine centuries before him, John XXIII urged his people to live their Catholic faith *more* purely, *more* deeply, *more* vigorously—not less. But unlike his medieval predecessor, John XXIII looked out on a world filled with promise. "The council now beginning," he said in his opening address, "rises in the Church like daybreak, a forerunner of most splendid light. It is now only dawn. And already at this first announcement of the rising day, how much sweetness fills our heart."

7.

WHAT WENT WRONG

HISTORY HAS A DARK sense of irony. John XXIII's new dawn for the church seemed to disappear like a mist as the 1960s ended.

Barely five years after the council closed, an uneasy Joseph Ratzinger wrote, "[We] are living at a tremendous turning point in the evolution of mankind, at a turning point compared with which the transition from Middle Ages to modern times seems as nothing." In the crush of drastic social and technological change, "the city of man is beginning to strike terror into our hearts."[1]

He soon followed with an essay soberly titled "Why I Am Still in the Church." In it, he surveyed the strife already sweeping the Catholic world. He wrote that "the Church is becoming extinguished in men's souls, and Christian communities are crumbling." In fact, "the Church now finds itself in a situation of Babylonian captivity, in which the 'for' and 'against' attitudes are not only tangled up in the oddest ways, but seem to allow scarcely any reconciliation. Mistrust has emerged, because being in the Church has lost straightforwardness, and no one any longer risks attributing honesty to another."[2]

He warned that

today an illusion is dangled before us: that a man can find himself without first conquering himself, without the patience of self denial and the labor of self control; that there is no need to endure the discomfort of upholding tradition, or to continue suffering the tension between the ideal and the actual in our nature. The presentation of this illusion constitutes the real crisis of our times. A man who has been relieved of all tribulation and led off into a never-never land has lost what makes him what he is; [he] has lost himself.[3]

The Fathers of Vatican II never imagined the struggles that followed the council. What went wrong?

Some answers seem clear. After years of relative Catholic peace, the council released explosive forces—both good and bad. Hopes for change in Catholic life, and for dialogue with the modern world, quickly became unrealistic. Confusion plagued many church leaders as Catholic intellectual life shifted. Politics and social science invaded the church's understanding of herself. The world applauded the changes in the church. But it demanded even more Catholic humility, relevance, and change. And it ignored the message of the church and her offers of partnership.[4] Laypeople grappled with new doubts—because if some things could change, maybe everything could. And if everything could change, maybe the church wasn't who she claimed to be.

Some critics have argued that Vatican II mistakenly downplayed the world's sinfulness. They claim it understated the need for Christ and his church as a remedy for the world's problems. Some see this as the main cause of the troubles that followed the council.[5] *Gaudium et Spes* often stands accused of an overly sunny view of human culture, a softness toward other faiths and even toward atheism. Yet even that document says:

> The Church believes that Christ, who died and was raised for all, can show man the way and strengthen him through the Spirit in order to be worthy of his destiny; nor is there any other name under heaven given among men by which they can be saved. The Church likewise believes that the key, the center and the purpose of the whole of man's history is to be found in its Lord and Master. She also maintains that beneath all that changes there is much that is unchanging, much that has its ultimate foundation in Christ, who is the same yesterday, and today, and forever (GS 10).

Outside forces also fed the confusion. The 1960s saw a turbulent mix of new social factors. After World War II, both Europe and America had great hopes for the future, despite millions dead in the war, the ongoing violence of communism, and poverty in the global South. Europe began overcoming its national hatreds. Largely through Christian Democratic leaders, Europeans moved toward creating the European Union. With Reverend Martin Luther King Jr. and others in the lead, Americans won civil rights for all citizens, regardless of color. Both continents grew wealthier. Both welcomed millions of immigrants. But World War II also left deep wounds that bred nihilism, extremism, and distrust for tradition and authority, along with consumer greed and naive beliefs about progress.

The church has always been skeptical of claims that mankind can find fulfillment this side of heaven. Still, after the council, many Catholics seemed to feel that human nature had somehow changed. For many, it no longer seemed so urgent to struggle against personal sin. Social progress was the real task for believers. Even the *idea* of limits seemed to fade.[6] True, certain kinds of limits did gain ground: limits on growth, population, corporations, and government. But the idea that wisdom begins with mastering our own *personal* appetites seemed to lose power.

Instead, the urge to reform social structures coexisted with huge optimism about the possibilities of personal joy, pleasure, freedom, and new forms of family and community. Scholars and some church leaders added to the confusion by claiming that the church would change her views on contraception and other inconvenient teachings. When that didn't happen, dashed hopes caused wider disputes. In the end, even the Catholic claim to have uniquely received the truth from Jesus Christ came under attack. As Joseph Ratzinger said in the mid-1980s, "In a world in which, at bottom, many believers are gripped by skepticism, the conviction of the Church that there is one truth, and that this one truth can as such be recognized, expressed and also clearly defined within certain bounds, appears scandalous."[7]

In America, Catholic upward mobility was too often not matched by real growth in the faith. Many Catholics who began attending the best universities ran into strong arguments against their faith for the first time. They were often ill-equipped with answers. While Catholics had great success in business, intellectual fields, and the professions, many wore their "Catholic" identity mainly as a cultural label. After the council, this led to a gulf between their professional and religious lives.

Even some who did seek Catholic higher learning received poor Catholic formation. Prior to Vatican II, American Catholic colleges and universities did well with limited resources. They may not have been at the cutting edge of research or intellectual life. But they offered good training in secular fields and strong undergraduate formation in Catholic philosophy, history, art, literature, and theology. When the 1960s hit the religious orders that ran many Catholic colleges, however, that foundation often gave way to very different thinking in psychology, social theory, and theology. Many of these intellectual experiments proved not only disappointing but destructive.

Other events in society shaped American Catholics. But none was greater than the arrival of chemical contraception in 1960. We should remember that all Christian churches held that contraception was morally wrong until the Anglican Church approved it in 1930 at the Lambeth Conference, though only for certain circumstances, and only within marriage.

Secular and religious leaders alike—among them Teddy Roosevelt, Sigmund Freud, and Mahatma Gandhi— had publicly criticized contraception. After Lambeth, many warned it would be impossible to restrict its use to married couples. They worried that marriage itself would suffer. The *Washington Post* editorialized at the time: "Carried to its logical conclusion, the [Lambeth] committee's report, if carried into effect, would sound the death knell of marriage as a holy institution by establishing degrading practices which would encourage indiscriminate immorality. The suggestion that the use of legalized contraception would be 'careful and restrained' is preposterous." The *Post* continued:

It is the misfortune of the churches that they are too often misused by visionaries for the promotion of "reforms" in fields foreign to religion. The departures from Christian teachings are astounding in many cases, leaving the beholder aghast at the unwillingness of some churches to teach "Christ and Him crucified." If the churches are to become organizations for political and scientific propaganda, they should be honest and reject the Bible, scoff at Christ as an obsolete and unscientific teacher, and strike out boldly as champions of politics and science as modern substitutes for the old-time religion.[8]

Those words from the *Washington Post* could equally describe the Catholic experience thirty years later, after Vatican II. Few disputed that Christians had historically seen contraception as violating God's command in Genesis to "be fruitful and multiply." And as events proved, contraception's toll on marriage, family, and society was massive. In the United States, it helped reshape sexual morality, led to higher divorce and illegitimacy rates, created pressure for legalized abortion, and coarsened male-female relations. But during and after the council, many American Catholics made contraception the decisive, borderline issue between a faith seemingly stuck in the past and one they felt was oriented to the future.

How a church without children could be "future oriented" was not explored.

Those who wanted change pushed it publicly. Reverend Charles Curran, a theologian at the Catholic University of America, led scores of religious figures to
dispute, in the pages of the *New York Times*, Pope Paul
VI's 1968 encyclical that reaffirmed Catholic teaching on
contraception. Curran was finally removed from the university. But it signaled trouble within the church herself
that partisans knew how to use the secular media and had
the will to do so.

Vatican II was the first church council to take place
on the global stage. In 1960, the mass media were often
ignorant of, or unfriendly to, Catholic beliefs. They often
framed conciliar issues as a morality tale pitting conservative troglodytes against reformers. Under the pen name
"Xavier Rynne," Francis Xavier Murphy, a Redemptorist
priest, wrote a series of "Letters from Vatican City" published by the *New Yorker* magazine. His work reinforced a
political model of conciliar conflict as the debates un-
folded. It also fed the presumptions of the American
Protestant and secular establishments, which arguably
had an interest in magnifying the council's progressives
and dismissing its more traditional elements. And this
model of "good progressives, bad traditionalists" persists
in media coverage to this day. When Benedict XVI issued
an apostolic exhortation in February 2007, much of the
press reported it as a document reasserting church beliefs

on abortion, contraception, euthanasia, and celibate priests—without noting that the *real* subject was the Eucharist.[9]

Spinning Vatican II as a sociological and political event continued in the council's aftermath. One of the more peculiar portraits was that of John XXIII himself—that is, the pope as indulgent Italian grandfather. More than forty years after John's death, aging Catholics still cling to the idea that, had John XXIII lived, the council would have changed so much more about the church. Alternately, some traditionalists see him as an evil genius who almost wrecked the faith.

No evidence supports any of this. John's love for the virtue of obedience would not have fit peacefully with the rebellion of later Catholic events. John was clearly a saintly man and an extraordinary pastor. But sometimes, hidden in people's nostalgia for John XXIII, is a presumption that God really had little to do with the actual council results, and that later popes disappointed John's vision. John XXIII would have found such views deeply troubling because they reveal a distrust for the church he loved. In fact, in the postconciliar debates about Vatican II, John's actual words have sometimes been ignored or interpreted to suggest the opposite of what he meant.

The council texts are so clear that persons who want to repurpose them often claim that pressure by the pope or Roman Curia stopped Vatican II from going farther. But the only authentic guide we have to the path proposed by the council fathers is the words they finally approved. The Catholic faith rests on its continuity with Jesus Christ, the Apostles, and the church they founded. Vatican II reflects that. And this continuity is exactly what stymies some Catholics who would prefer the church to be something other than she is. Joseph Ratzinger once lamented that by 1973, many of his former theological allies already felt that the council was not drastic enough. They dismissed it as the work of an old clerical culture.[10]

Examples of this dictatorship of the interpreters surface in many discussions of Vatican II. The most misleading is the argument that Catholics have no special claim to God's truth; that all religions lead in roughly equal ways to God. *Nostra Aetate*, the text on Catholic relations with non-Christians, is often cited to support this view. The trouble is, *Nostra Aetate* explicitly *reaffirms* Catholic belief in the unique role of Jesus Christ for all humanity and the unique mission of the Catholic Church.[11]

Many skills exist—scientific, economic, and political—that the Catholic Church as such does not possess. No sensible Catholic leader would say otherwise. But the church *does* claim that she was entrusted by Jesus Christ with the truths needed for salvation. The church has much in common with both Jews and other Christian communities. The council therefore urges respect among all those who share a role in salvation history. The church even seeks dialogue with faiths beyond the biblical horizon. But she never forgets the central role of Jesus Christ. *Nostra Aetate* sought to go beyond the polemics of the past and to build cooperation where possible—nothing less, but also nothing more.

Today, the misreading of *Nostra Aetate* often combines with a poor grasp of *Dignitatis Humanae*, the council's Declaration on Religious Liberty. In the past, the church had often opposed the notion that non-Catholic religions had the right to public expression. Vatican II profoundly changed the Catholic approach to this issue.

Yet the Catholic faith does not hold, and Vatican II did not teach, that respect for conscience means that individuals have absolute sovereignty in determining their own truth, or that anyone's choice of beliefs is as good as any other. Even the secular order admits that some choices are good and others bad. Whatever we may tolerate, every person has duties to seek and serve the truth: "Religious freedom, in turn, which men demand as necessary to fulfill their duty to worship God, has to do with immunity from coercion in civil society. Therefore *it leaves untouched traditional Catholic doctrine on the moral duty of men and societies toward the true religion and toward the one Church of Christ*" (DH 1; emphasis added).

Dignitatis Humanae noted that the church in the past had failed in her duty to respect other people's consciences: "In the life of the People of God, as it has made its pilgrim way through the vicissitudes of human history, there has at times appeared a way of acting that was hardly in accord with the spirit of the Gospel or even opposed to it. Nevertheless, the doctrine of the Church that no one is to be coerced into faith has always stood firm" (DH 12).

Yet the same text also stressed that all persons have the duty "to form their own judgments in the light of truth" (DH 7). It also reminded Catholics that "the faithful must pay careful attention to the sacred and certain teaching of the Church. For the Catholic Church is, by the will of Christ, the teacher of truth" (DH 14).

Like *Dignitatis Humanae*, few texts are more of an icon for Vatican II than *Gaudium et Spes*, the Pastoral Constitution on the Church in the Modern World. The longest of the conciliar documents, it was also the most heavily discussed and edited. In the council's last session, more than twenty thousand amendments to the text were proposed. A reader today can see in the document a generous desire to positively engage the modern world, something the church had often failed to do in the nineteenth and early twentieth centuries.

That earlier Catholic resistance to modern thought was caused by the persecution of the church after the French Revolution and fears that popular governments elsewhere might do the same. Indeed, Pope Pius IX, who served as pope from 1846 to 1878, entered office as something of a liberal reformer. He allowed a democratic opening in the Papal States until his prime minister, Pel-

legrino Rossi, was murdered by extremists in 1848. Pius
had to be smuggled out of Rome to escape being killed.
That event marked him deeply. It led Pius to famously
say in his *Syllabus of Errors* that it was *delirementa* (mad-
ness) to believe "the Roman Pontiff can and should reconcile himself to and agree with progress, liberalism and
modern civilization." But Pius was no simple reactionary.
He was shaped by real threats.

Gaudium et Spes can be seen as a readjustment, a development in the Catholic understanding of how to relate
to the new public order. Ratzinger put it this way:

> If one is looking for a global diagnosis of the text
> [of *Gaudium et Spes*], one could say that it (along
> with the texts on religious liberty and world reli-
> gions) is a revision of the Syllabus of Pius IX, a
> kind of counter-Syllabus . . . Let us content our-
> selves here with stating that the text [of *Gaudium et
> Spes*] plays the role of a counter-Syllabus to the ex-
> tent that it represents an attempt to officially rec-
> oncile the Church with the world as it had become
> after 1789 . . . "World" is understood here, in
> depth, as the spirit of modern times. The Church's
> consciousness of being a distinct group regarded
> this spirit as something separate from herself and,
> after the hot as well as cold wars were over, she
> sought dialogue and cooperation with it.[12]

But a more common reading of the text—in fact, a distortion—is to look at *Gaudium et Spes* as giving priority to Christian engagement with the *political* world, as if the old stress on personal reform were merely a prelude to the maturity of the modern age. Worse, this shift away from the old struggles of "personal morality" can have the effect of implying that people are simply the products of social structures. Thus, any faults we have are excusable facts of our natures. In America, this has grown into a cult of self-esteem and an unwillingness to judge. It's now hard to claim that anything *anyone* does, anywhere, is inherently wrong. As one observer said, *Gaudium et Spes* actually *upholds* the old personal morality, and in doing so, exalts human beings: "The view of man that is ascendant in American society today is not one that thinks too much of man, but too little."[13]

Properly understood, these council texts welcome the good in modern, pluralistic societies but not the extremes to which free societies tend. Common sense and daily experience suggest that any society that accepts all moral views as having equal weight is headed for trouble. A nation like the United States is rooted in a basic understanding of God-given rights but also in the limits God places on our freedoms. Take away these foundational beliefs, and the whole system weakens. Just prior to his election as pope, Cardinal Ratzinger warned against the "dictatorship of relativism," which he sees as the main threat to free societies in our time. In its balancing of the need for freedom and the need to live according to the truth, Vatican II reflected classic Catholic wisdom about human life.

Two young Catholic leaders at the council embodied this balance. Both were later accused of turning "conservative" as they grew older. Karol Wojtyla, later Pope John Paul II, helped sponsor the document on religious liberty. He knew from experience that religious freedom needed protection against repressive states. Joseph Ratzinger, later Pope Benedict XVI, pressed for greater zeal in preaching the Gospel and against unhealthy Catholic inertia and formalism. Both men saw their ideas as an answer to modern circumstances. Wojtyla knew that authentic Catholic faith needed a strong defense from the misuses of freedom. And Ratzinger saw enough mistakes in the name of reform that he soon broke with the more radical views of former colleagues. Neither man turned his back on the task of renewal. Neither man abandoned his own youthful insights. Rather, each resisted changes that veered away from the Catholic tradition.

In America, the council took place in the shadow of U.S. global power, postwar material success, and the end of ghetto Catholicism. John F. Kennedy's election as president in 1960 culminated a long, uneven history for American Catholics. Kennedy was young, charismatic, and decisive. In the new media world shaped by television, these were vital qualities. His wife, Jacqueline, brought to Washington an elegance that equaled any previous presidency. The Kennedys ended any notion that Catholics were second-class citizens.

Prior to Kennedy, only one other Catholic layman, New York governor Al Smith, had run for the presidency. In 1928, he had lost in a wave of anti-Catholic bigotry. But Catholics had largely found a place in American society by the 1960s. They were eager to see themselves as Americans. John Kennedy was an icon for that process: He came from a wealthy family, was publicly Catholic, went to Harvard, and served the country as a PT boat captain in World War II.

Even so, Kennedy had problems on his way to the White House. His campaign ran into latent—and sometimes quite open—anti-Catholic fears. In a speech to the Greater Houston Ministerial Association on September 12, 1960, Kennedy made it clear that, as president, he would not take orders from the Vatican or the American bishops.[14] This was a defensible view, especially at the time, since few public policy issues directly troubled Catholic faith or morals. Catholic leaders in Europe had not run afoul of the Holy See or local bishops after World War II. Kennedy noted Charles de Gaulle in France and Konrad Adenauer in Germany as examples.

But in an effort to be as "American" as the Protestants he was addressing, Kennedy clouded the waters:

I believe in an America where the separation of church and state is absolute—where no Catholic

prelate would tell the President (should he be
Catholic) how to act, and no Protestant minister
would tell his parishioners for whom to vote—
where no church or church school is granted any
public funds or political preference—and where no
man is denied public office merely because his religion differs from the President who might ap-
point him or the people who might elect him.[15]

This was shrewd politics. But it also had very deep
implications. One historian remarked, "The joke was
that [Kennedy] turned out to be, in effect, our first Baptist president—one, that is, who defended a thorough-
going separation more characteristic of that group than
of his own church."[16]

Even in classic Catholic thought, the church must respect the institutions of the state. But when church leaders refrain from helping political leaders see their moral
responsibilities, their lack of action implies that religion
has nothing to say to the public square. So eager was
Kennedy to dispel fears of Catholic control that he said
precisely that:

I believe in an America that is officially neither
Catholic, Protestant nor Jewish—where no public
official either requests or accepts instructions on
public policy from the Pope, the National Council
of Churches or any other ecclesiastical source—

where no religious body seeks to impose its will
directly or indirectly upon the general populace or
the public acts of its officials—and where religious
liberty is so indivisible that an act against one
church is treated as an act against all.

Again, this was good rhetoric, and Kennedy probably
spoke for a new majority of American Catholics. But in
playing to his audience's old fears of Roman inter-
ference—"instructions on public policy from the Pope"—
his words stripped the public square of religious influence
and attacked the principle of pluralism and free speech.
Church and state are rightly separate. Both religion and
politics, however, address the question of how to live in
the world. They *always* influence each other, and should.

Kennedy did make one important statement about
his faith: "But if the time should ever come—and I do
not concede any conflict to be even remotely possible—
when my office would require me to either violate my
conscience or violate the national interest, then I would
resign the office; and I hope any conscientious public servant would do the same."

In his Houston speech, Kennedy wanted to stress his
commitment to conscience, but he vastly underestimated
the impact of his remarks. The American Jesuit John
Courtney Murray reportedly warned that "to make religion merely a private matter was idiocy," and he later
wrote in a 1967 letter to a friend that Kennedy had been

"far more of a separationist than I am."[17] Another Catholic commentator went even further: "Kennedy seemed to suggest that religion is fine for a politician so long as it's merely personal; though maybe it shouldn't be too personal for him, either."

Few people today would expect even the most pious Catholic public official to "take orders" from the American bishops or the Holy See. But the questions raised by Vatican II for Catholic identity and American politics are very far from over. In fact, our political vocabulary has never been more marked than it is today by a civil war over the meaning of words and ideas.

When we look back over the past four decades, Vatican II may have assumed a maturity and zeal in Catholics that too few of us have lived—or even understood. Many Catholics who invoke the council to defend personal conscience and religious liberty seem to have little grasp of what the council actually meant about either of those issues. And too often in the United States, Catholic thought since the council has not been a child of Vatican II, but of American political and popular culture. In fact, too many of us have become *evangelizers* in the most ironic sense of the word: preaching the world to a church we claim to love, but which we no longer really understand.

8.

CONSCIENCE AND COWARDICE

STEPHEN COLBERT, THE YOUNGEST of eleven children from an Irish Catholic family, created one of the shrewdest political satire television shows in recent years, *The Colbert Report.*

In his first appearance, Colbert launched the show's trademark word: *truthiness.* He put it this way:

> Now I'm sure some of the word police, the *word-anistas* over at Webster's, are gonna say, "Hey, that's not a word." Well, anybody who knows me knows that I am no fan of dictionaries or reference books. They're elitist, constantly telling us what is or isn't true; or what did or didn't happen . . . I don't trust books. They're all fact, no heart. And that's exactly what's pulling our country apart today. Because face it, folks, we are a divided nation. Not between Democrats or Republicans, or conservatives and liberals, or tops and bottoms. No,

> we are divided between those who *think* with their
> head, and those who *know* with their heart . . . The
> truthiness is, anyone can read the news to you. I
> promise to *feel* the news *at* you.[1]

Speaking out of character about modern political debate, Colbert later said: "It used to be, everyone was en-
titled to their own opinion, but not their own facts. But
that's not the case anymore. Facts matter not at all. Perception is everything . . . I really feel a dichotomy in the
American populace. What is important? What you *want*
to be true, or what *is* true?" He added: "Truthiness is,
'What I say is right, and [nothing] anyone else says could
possibly be true.' It's not only that I *feel* it to be true, but
that *I* feel it to be true. There's not only an emotional
quality, but there's a selfish quality."[2]

People laugh because Colbert is right. Once upon a
time, words had weight. Now they float. In the past,
Americans understood equality as something basic that
we all share before God and the law. Now it means that
almost everyone feels anointed to have his or her views
taken seriously, no matter how unfettered by fact, logic,
civility, or common sense. Unfortunately, experience
teaches the opposite. Some ideas are bad. Some opinions
are foolish. Some feelings are vindictive. And some people lie. The American genius for marketing, however, is
a neutral skill. It can sell sand in a desert, and cigarettes
just as artfully as vitamins. So it becomes very important

for citizens to *think* their politics, not feel them; to examine the language of public discourse for what the words really mean.

In his essay "Politics and the English Language" (1946), George Orwell observed that "one ought to recognize that the present political chaos is connected with the decay of language, and that one can probably bring about some improvement by starting at the verbal end."[3] Writing at the close of a world war that killed more than 30 million people, Orwell warned that the deliberate abuse of language had played a big role in the political collapse the world then suffered. If Joseph Stalin could claim to be a "democrat," the word meant nothing at all; or even worse, the *opposite* of its original meaning. Orwell argued that, in the modern era, political language has become mainly a tool to obscure or defend the indefensible.

Orwell knew that words have power because they convey meaning. Words shape our thinking, which shapes our actions. Dishonest public debate with its misuse of words leads to bad laws and dangerous politics. When the meaning of a word is subverted, it acts like a virus. It infects other words and ideas. It spreads the habit of adjusting the facts and what they mean to serve predetermined political ends. In a different age, we called this lying. Now we call it spin. But whatever we name it, voter cynicism and a weaker democratic life are the result.

Massaging the facts to get elected—what candidates

call "framing the issues"—is hardly new to American politics. It goes with the messiness of an open society. This is why George Washington and other founders spoke so forcefully about the need for a literate, educated citizenry. Democratic life depends on a people with the reasoning skills to see through the chicanery that often goes with political debate.

The new mass media that shape our views, however, have much more power than in the past. Americans now spend large parts of the day watching television, listening to the radio, or exploring the Internet. More books than ever are in print, but serious reading has declined. This has *political* implications. Just as the American idea of human rights depends on a vocabulary shaped historically by religion, so does our political process depend on an ability to judge and reason shaped by the printed word and the culture it helped create. Reading cultivates the skills of abstract thought, mental acuity, and attention to the logical structure of a sentence. At its best, reading breeds an *appropriately* critical mind; that is, a mind able to sustain focus, judge information, imagine alternatives, and choose logically. It's no accident that Tocqueville noticed two striking qualities about the newly independent Americans: their religious practice and their love of the printed word.

This doesn't mean that electronic media are bad. In any case, we can't avoid them. But it does mean that we need to develop what Bertrand Russell called an "immunity to eloquence" as we experience them. In other words, we should know how the media work, and especially how they work *on us*. The "eloquence" of the new electronic media is their entertainment effect: their stress on brevity, energy, variety, emotion, and visual imagery. We need to remember that the *form* of information is part of its content. As Neil Postman once observed, every new information medium is "not merely a machine but a structure for discourse, which both rules out and insists upon certain kinds of content and, inevitably, a certain kind of audience."[4] The new media breed and feed an audience—including voters—with little patience for complexity or sustained debate.

This is exactly the opposite of early American civic literacy. In the postcolonial years, most ordinary people not only could read and *did* read but eagerly joined in political debate. When Alexander Hamilton, James Madison, and John Jay wrote *The Federalist Papers*, they already knew that an educated citizenry *wanted* to read and debate them. A culture like this forms minds that can retain and weigh large amounts of conceptual information; minds able to follow arguments—even dense and abstract ones.

In an electronic culture, vast chunks of incoming information have no importance at all. They simply gum up our ability to distinguish and rank issues. Politics tends to dumb down into what Christopher Lasch called "ideological gestures." A serious marketplace of ideas, a place where opposing views get fairly debated and the best course of action emerges as the winner, simply can't survive in a climate ruled by the sound bite. "The problem," Neil Postman wrote, "is not that television presents us with entertaining subject matter, but that all subject matter is presented as entertaining."[5] Crime, war, public humiliation, sexual intimacy, pain, and political leadership—much of our experience of these things comes from watching them on network shows. We begin to judge their value by how prevalent they are on television and how well they hold our attention there.

The new media have two other key flaws. First, in their immersive effect, they obscure the large amounts of important information they *don't* communicate. The need for brevity creates an artificial need for simplicity. Facts that don't fit within the forms or appetites of the media often get ignored. But the real world, including human motives, is a huge and tangled place. Thus, despite a modern tidal wave of certain *kinds* of data, we actually live in what Bill McKibben famously described as an Un-Enlightenment, an age of missing information.[6]

Second, in their persuasive effect, the new media instruct the public on how to think and what they need. Some of this subtle tutoring can be funny, especially in advertising. It led Neil Postman to see American television commercials as a form of "religious parables, organized around a coherent theology. Like all religious parables, [television commercials] put forward a concept of sin, intimations of the way to redemption, and a vision of Heaven. They also suggest what are the roots of evil, and what are the obligations of the holy."[7] George Orwell put it more bluntly when he equated consumer advertising with "the banging of a spoon in a swill bucket," but the point is that selling a product, an idea, or a political candidate requires much the same skill set. Even major print-news organizations, while paying lip service to fairness, tend to frame complex stories in a streamlined and ideologically loaded way.

When Orwell wrote his 1946 essay on the political debasement of language, he spoke to a culture that was still largely *typographic*; that had been formed by the mental disciplines of print. The English language today has vastly more power because of the new technologies that carry it. Those same tools make it easier to mislead, confuse, and lie to citizens, and then coach them to smile while they're being robbed.

" 'WHEN I USE a word,' Humpty Dumpty said in rather a scornful tone, 'it means just what I choose it to mean—neither more nor less.' " Lewis Carroll wrote those words more than a century ago in *Through the Looking Glass*, but Humpty Dumpty might do very well in public office today. Dissembling in political life is now a national habit. Mass media tools make it easy. If we love our country—and we have that duty as citizens—we

must try to recover and insist on the real meaning of ou
public vocabulary. *Truth, pluralism, consensus, choice, the
common good, democracy, conscience, love, equal rights, tolerance*—all of these words are now routinely misused in
public debate to serve selfish or destructive ends.

Pluralism is a demographic fact. Nothing more. It is
not a philosophy or ideology or secular cult. It does not
imply that all ideas and religious beliefs are equally
valid, because they're not. We live in a diverse country.
That requires us to treat each other with respect. This
makes sense both morally and pragmatically. But "pluralism" does not require us to mute our convictions. Nor
does it *ever* excuse us from speaking and acting to advance
our beliefs about justice and the common good in public.
Catholics who use "pluralism" as an alibi for their public
inaction suffer from what the early church described as
dypsychia. In other words, they're ruled by two conflict-
ing spirits. They may speak like disciples, but their unwillingness to act paralyzes their words.

Tolerance is a working principle that enables us to live
in peace with other people and their ideas. Most of the
time, it's a very good thing. But it is not an end in itself,
and tolerating or excusing grave evil in a society is itself
a grave evil. The roots of this word are revealing. *Tolerance* comes from the Latin *tolerare*, "to bear or sustain,"
and *tollere*, which means "to lift up." It implies bearing
other persons and their beliefs the way we carry a burden
or endure a headache. It's actually a negative idea. And it

is not a Christian virtue. Catholics have the duty not to "tolerate" other people but to love them, which is a much more demanding task. Justice, charity, mercy, courage, wisdom—these are Christian virtues; but not tolerance. Prudence too is a vital Christian virtue, the "right rudder of reason," but not when we use it as a cover for political cowardice. Real Christian virtues flow from an understanding of truth, unchanging and rooted in God, that exists and obligates us whether we like it or not. The pragmatic social truce we call "tolerance" has no such grounding.

In like manner, building a *consensus* around laws and policies is usually a worthy goal. But whether such a consensus is good or evil depends on the content of the specific laws and policies. A *consensus*—which simply means the "agreement of the people"—is never a source of truth. It says nothing at all about whether a policy is good or a law is evil. In fact, a consensus is often wrong. A great many unjust wars and bad leaders have been very popular.

And this leads us to another brutalized word, *democracy*, which couples the Greek words *demos* (people) and *kratos* (power). Switzerland and North Korea both claim to be democracies. The latter's official name is the People's Democratic Republic of Korea. In the United States, however, *democracy* means "majority rule by the citizens through representative, constitutional government." American democracy does *not* ask its citizens to put aside their deeply held moral and religious beliefs for the sake of public policy. In fact, *it requires exactly the opposite.* People are fallible. The majority of voters can be uninformed or biased or simply wrong. Thus, to survive, American democracy depends on people of character fighting for their beliefs in the public square—legally, ethically, and nonviolently, but forcefully and without apology. Anything less is a form of theft from the nation's health.

Other key words in our political conversation suffer from the same vocabulary drift. *Choice* is worthless—in fact, it's a form of idolatry—if all the choices are meaningless or bad. Our basic *rights* don't emerge or exist in a vacuum. They come to us as endowments from our Creator, and we have obligations that go along with them. *Community* is more than a collection of persons with the same appetites or complaints. A real community requires mutual respect, a shared past and future, and submission to each other's needs based on common beliefs and principles. It is not an elegant name for an interest group.

Nor is the *common good* merely the sum of what most people want right now. The "common good" is that which constitutes the best source of justice and happiness for a community and its members *in the light of truth.* In the mind of the Second Vatican Council, it includes all those conditions of social life that enable individuals, families, and organizations to achieve their true fulfillment (GS 74). This "true fulfillment" presumes that external, fundamental truths about human nature and meaning preexist us. We don't invent those truths.

Finally *conscience*, as Cardinal Newman once said, "has rights because it has duties."[8] In Newman's words, "We can believe what we choose. We are answerable for what we choose to believe."[9] As Catholics, we must act according to our conscience. But we should also remember that we all have great skill at self-deception when it suits us. Conscience is never merely a matter of personal preference or opinion. Nor is it a self-esteem coach. It is a gift of God; the strong, still, uncomfortably honest voice inside us that speaks the truth if we let it. In fact, to continue with Newman,

> the more a person tries to obey his conscience, the more he gets alarmed with himself for obeying it so imperfectly . . . But next, while he grows in self-knowledge, he also understands more and more clearly that the voice of conscience has nothing gentle, nothing of mercy in its tone. It is severe and even stern. It does not speak of forgiveness, but of punishment. It suggests to him a future judgment; it does not tell him how he can avoid it.[10]

Conscience has the task of telling us the hard truth about our actions. The *church* has the task of expressing God's love and leading us to salvation. For Catholics, "conscience" demands a mind and heart well formed in the truth of Jesus Christ. And these come foremost through the teaching of the Catholic faith.

Obviously, faith is not a mathematical equation. People often face difficult issues in daily life. Some Catholics may find themselves sincerely unable, in conscience, to accept a point of Catholic teaching. When that happens, the test of a believer's honesty is his humility; that is, his willingness to put the matter to real prayer and the seriousness of his effort to accept the wisdom of the church and follow her guidance. If after this effort he still cannot reconcile himself with the teaching of the church, he must do what he believes to be right, because ultimately, every Catholic must follow his or her conscience. At the same time, we should remember that honest private decisions—the kind that come from hard self-examination—are very different from the organized, premeditated, public rejection of Catholic belief by persons who use their Catholic identity to attack what the Catholic faith holds as true.

Organized dissent in the name of "conscience," especially in a media age that celebrates almost anyone who challenges authority, very easily—and much too conveniently—lends itself to vanity and evasion. It tribalizes Catholic life by turning the church into a battleground for interest groups and personal ego. In fact, one of the saddest qualities of the current American Catholic scene is that, when it comes to the meaning of *Catholic*, quite a few of us are Lewis Carroll fans without knowing it.

" 'When I use a word,' Humpty Dumpty said in rather a scornful tone, 'it means *just what I choose it to mean*—neither more nor less.' "

JOHN COURTNEY MURRAY once raised the question of whether Americans still really believe in the American Proposition. This "proposition" holds that the United States was founded on certain basic truths. Humanity knows these truths not only through religious faith but through reason and experience. And these truths remain true whether one personally believes them or not.

Murray had little sympathy for the secularism of his day. He understood the difference between nonsectarian public life and the modern, secularist contempt for religious faith. In the decade before Vatican II, Murray spent much of his time in controversy with a scholar named Paul Blanshard. Blanshard wrote a book in 1949 called *American Freedom and Catholic Power*. In it, Blanshard attacked the Catholic Church, calling it "a state within a state and above a state." Blanshard feared the growing Catholic influence in American life. He argued that the church's only aim was to strengthen her own power. In practice, for Blanshard, a Catholic could not be genuinely "Catholic" and also genuinely American.

Blanshard's ideas were not new. They were the usual, tired, overwrought fears of Catholic papism repackaged for a new generation. But what most concerned Murray was Blanshard's technique. He had wrapped his new attacks not in Protestant but secularist garb. Murray grasped that if Blanshard were successful, Catholics wouldn't be the only exiles ejected from the public square; *all* religiously grounded values would soon follow them out.[11]

Murray argued that the truths of the American Proposition "were not the original product of the Enlightenment and its American Deist heirs, but of the Catholic medieval theory of man and society." Murray saw that Blanshard's views threatened not just Catholics but anyone who believed "that democracy had something to do with transcendent values." In *We Hold These Truths*, he wrote that Blanshard's anti-Catholicism pushed a political theory in which "the noble, many storeyed mansion of democracy [would] be dismantled, leveled to the dimensions of a flat majoritarianism, which is no mansion but a barn, perhaps even a tool shed in which the weapons of tyranny may be formed."[12]

Murray believed that no compromise could be reached with such a prospect. He knew that secularists are as committed to their beliefs as serious Catholics are to theirs. He wrote that the secularist "is at war. If he knows his own history, he must be. Historically his first chosen enemy was the Catholic Church, and it must still be the Enemy of his choice."[13]

Why would this be so? For two reasons. In Murray's words:

First, [the Catholic Church] asserts that there is an authority superior to the authority of individual reason and of the political projection of individual reason, the state . . . Second, it asserts that by divine ordinance this world is to be ruled by a diarchy of authorities, within which the temporal is subordinate to the spiritual, not instrumentally but in dignity . . . [yet in] secularist theory there can only be one society, one law, one power and one faith, a civic faith that is the "unifying" faith bond of the community, whereby it withstands the assaults of assorted pluralisms . . . What alarms [the secularist] is religion as a Thing, visible, corporate, organized, a community of thought that presumes to sit superior to, and in judgment on, the "community of democratic thought," and that is furnished somehow with an armature of power to make its thought and judgment publicly prevail.[14]

Murray understood secularist reasoning, but he saw that a public square stripped of religious influence invited a new kind of barbarism, and this danger required from Christians a political response rooted in courage. In fact, even with his impressive intellectual credentials, Murray believed that the virtue of courage is as vitally important as intelligence, if not more so. Humans live their personal and social lives "close to the brink of barbarism, threatened . . . by the decadence of moral corruption and the political chaos of formlessness or the moral chaos of tyranny. Society is rescued from chaos only by a few men, not by the many."[15] The few are those courageous persons who struggle on behalf of moral convictions that serve the common good.

Murray resisted the relatively mild American secularism of the 1950s and 1960s, so he might be stunned by our political environment today. He built his life's work on the importance of the church recognizing religious liberty as a "most basic human right." But he also saw the need for American Catholics to develop a new and genuine religious maturity; a maturity that would respect the freedom of persons to do as they choose within the limits of the common welfare, but which would also infuse them with the fidelity and courage to choose what they knew, through their Catholic faith and reason, to be *right*.

That same need for Catholic maturity is even more urgent today. As Catholics and citizens, we need to cultivate the ability to distinguish between legitimate compromise and cowardice; between prudence and weakness in ourselves and our elected officials. Compromise often helps the political process to achieve progress. In the United States, the law currently allows abortion on demand. We live under that unjust law, but we sin only if we give up the struggle to change it. Room exists for gradualism along the way. But the direct killing of unborn children is gravely evil, without exception. No alibis can excuse it. The law must be changed.

Neutrality and dissembling on grave moral issues never finally work. In their public speaking, John F. Kennedy and Winston Churchill both quoted Dante's *Divine Comedy* to the effect that "the hottest place in hell is reserved for those who in times of great moral crisis maintained their neutrality." Actually the source of the quotation is unknown; it appears nowhere in the *Divine Comedy*. In the *Inferno*, Dante does depict where cowards and neutrals spend their eternity: neither in heaven *nor* in hell, because neither place wants them. Dante's famous road map to eternity is of course poetic, not literal church teaching. But his point about the cowardice and selfishness of moral neutrality, and where they lead, sounds alarmingly accurate: God did not put us here to sit out the struggle for the soul of the public square.

We need to remember John Courtney Murray's emphasis on the need for courage. In fact, Catholics can take a lesson in the courage to follow a well-formed Christian conscience from Dr. Martin Luther King Jr. King was first and above all a Christian minister, guided by his faith in Jesus Christ. His "Letter from Birmingham Jail" is an actual letter; a response to Alabama clergymen who publicly criticized King for interfering in local affairs, pushing for human rights, and breaking the law while arguing other laws were unjust.[16]

The clergymen wanted to know why King, an outsider, had come to Birmingham in the first place. King answered that he came because injustice was there. He argued that he could not sit idly by in Atlanta and ignore evil events in Birmingham. Injustice anywhere, felt King, is a threat to justice everywhere. People are linked in an inescapable network of mutuality, a single garment of destiny: "Whatever affects one directly, affects all indirectly." King felt *compelled* to be in Birmingham. To stay in Atlanta would have violated his sense of what was just and morally necessary.

King then addressed the "troublemaker" charges leveled against him: "I must confess that I am not afraid of the word 'tension.' I have earnestly opposed violent tension, but there is a type of constructive, nonviolent tension which is necessary for growth." He was not naive. He did not assume that progress would happen without human choice, action, and sacrifice. Human history was not set on an automatic pilot to expand justice, freedom, and equality under the law to all peoples. Certain people would need to create tension to push progress forward.

King's "weapon of nonviolence" required him and his followers to willfully disobey unjust laws and accept the legal consequences. He knew that when a critical mass of his followers accepted the cost of changing bad laws, a tipping point would be reached, and events would turn in his favor.

King believed that "one has a moral responsibility to disobey unjust laws." In his "Letter," he invoked two great doctors of the Christian church, Augustine and Thomas Aquinas. He argued that "a just law is a man-made code that squares with the moral law or the law of God. An unjust law is a code that is out of harmony with the moral law." King did not advocate breaking the law only because it was unjust, but also to teach a lesson. A person who breaks the law must also have a "willingness to accept the penalty. I submit that an individual who breaks a law that conscience tells him is unjust and who willingly accepts the penalty of imprisonment in order to arouse the conscience of the community over its injustice, is in reality expressing the highest respect for law."

King wrote at length in his "Letter" about the kind of citizen he considered almost worse than the "rabid segregationist"—the "white moderate." White moderates were citizens who agreed with his goals personally but refused to support his public actions. He wrote that he had hoped that the "white moderate would understand that law and order exist for the purpose of establishing justice, and that when they fail in this purpose they become the dangerously structured dams that block the flow of social progress." His hope had often been disappointed.

Dr. King and his followers were willing to go to jail for conscience' sake. His "Letter" is an example of using language in the service of truth; of the power of words to compel action consistent with God's higher law; of a healthy and articulate Christian conscience. His "Letter" also reminds us that too many of us are willing to live quite comfortably as cowards. King wrote that "human progress never rolls in on wheels of inevitability; it comes through the tireless efforts of men willing to be co-workers with God, and without this hard work, time itself becomes an ally of the forces of social stagnation."

King was deeply troubled that the world so readily dismissed the Christian church, Christ's community of disciples, "as an irrelevant social club with no meaning for the 20th century." He lamented, "In deep disappointment I have wept over the laxity of the Church." King had little use for lax Christians. Neither should we—especially if the lax Christians are us. We have no excuses. We have too many models of courage to guide us.

9.

A MAN FOR ALL SEASONS

Over the centuries, a great many saints and sinners have shaped the course of society. But the undisputed icon of the Catholic political vocation is the "heavenly patron of statesmen and politicians," as Pope John Paul II called him in 2000, Saint Thomas More.

Nearly five hundred years after his death, More is larger than life. He transcends time and culture. His witness endures today as strongly as it did in sixteenth-century England. In the words of G. K. Chesterton, Thomas More

is more important at this moment than at any moment since his death, even perhaps the great moment of his dying; but he is not quite so important as he will be in about a hundred years' time. He may come to be counted the greatest Englishman, or at least the greatest historical character in English history. For he was above all things historic;

he represented at once a type, a turning point and an ultimate destiny. If there had not happened to be that particular man at the particular moment, the whole of history would have been different.[1]

Anyone unfamiliar with More's life can simply watch the 1966 film version of Robert Bolt's play, *A Man for All Seasons*. It's a story of love and betrayal, of service and treachery, of a very human man trying to follow his conscience and the unsavory men responsible for his demise. But *why* does Thomas More still have such power? What is it about More's life and death that so many people feel drawn to?

More's appeal springs from the desire we all share to lead a life of conviction, courage, and love. Today we have plenty of talented, well-meaning public officials, but very few in the mold of More. Something basic seems lacking in American public life. Thomas More reminds us what that "something" is.

More stands as a witness against cowardice. He lived in interesting times not so alien to our own. He was a man of genuine Catholic faith at a moment when the assumptions that had sustained Christendom for centuries were unraveling into turmoil. He was also a humanist; a friend of Erasmus; a man of letters, prudence, and diplomacy. More had no illusions about the corruption of individual clerics, the lethargy and hypocrisy of too many church leaders, and the urgent need for church reform.

He also ably served King Henry VIII, whose policies he often felt were venal. He did not always agree with his sovereign. Nonetheless, once the king set a course, More complied with it. He did this with energy and ability, because among his core virtues was fidelity to duty. When the day came that service to his king clashed with what he held as a Catholic to be sacred, he betrayed neither his king nor his faith. He resigned.

More later stood trial for treason and was beheaded. The charges against him were false. More died having committed no crime. The Parliament had passed the Acts of Succession and Supremacy. These declared Henry VIII the head of the Church of England and denied the pope's authority. Because of his Catholic faith, More could not accept the actions of Parliament and the king. But as a skillful lawyer and politician, he also hoped that if he remained silent about the acts, no one could justly accuse him of any crime. More was wrong. He was accused and found guilty on false testimony from people bent on forcing More to publicly support the king's claims.

Why did More's silence speak so loudly? Why did his peers *need* him to publicly endorse Henry's divorce from Catherine of Aragon, marriage to Anne Boleyn, and power over the church? Why did anyone care what Thomas More thought in the first place? And why does anyone care now?

The answer is character. Then, as now, fidelity to

principle was worth more than gold. People knew from experience that Thomas More was a man of his word; a man of honor in his public service and holiness in his private life. More did not inherit these qualities. He worked to achieve them. In doing so, he stood in vivid contrast to the man he replaced as England's lord chancellor: Cardinal Thomas Wolsey. Both men were gifted public officials. Both men loved the church. But Wolsey—an embodiment of the powerful, late Renaissance prelate— would morally compromise himself in ways that More could not and did not. More understood his times, his choices, and their implications far more clearly than Wolsey ever did.[2] And the virtues that More would exemplify as lord chancellor would come to distinguish the man we still remember today.

More would often tell his children that "we cannot go to heaven in featherbeds." He practiced what he preached. More worked hard to rein in his quick tongue and prideful ambitions. He brought the same unblinkered realism to judging his own sins that he used in understanding the world around him. As a result, he disciplined himself to be a man of piety. His morning prayer and Mass routine, his fasting and hair shirt, have become symbols of his devotion. But we should never forget that these outward signs merely gave proof to the inner man who committed his whole life to Jesus Christ and Christ's church.

From an early age, More grasped the need not merely to study and talk about God but to *love* God and to allow him to transform the heart. As a young adult, More lived for a time with monks, discerning whether God would call him to the priesthood or to marriage. Public officials today often seem uneasy in talking about their religious faith. But such behavior would have baffled More and the people of his day. More knew that the very idea of "vocation" flows from the assumption that a loving God with a plan for all of us exists; a God who calls each of us to a special task. Thus, More sought to serve God above all things; not "God" as a pious ideal but as a living, personal Reality. In one of his early books, *The Life of John Picus*, More stated, "For if a man had God always before his eyes as a ruler of all his works, and in all his works should neither seek his own lucre, his glory, nor his own pleasure, but only the pleasure of God, he should shortly be perfect."

The grandson and son of prominent London lawyers, More learned very early the honor in serving one's nation. More's studies prepared him for a life of public service, primarily in law. But his education also included the classics: the ancient Greeks, Romans, and early church fathers; philosophy, theology, history, and literature. More had an adroit, sophisticated mind. He had a shrewd insight into human nature, political society, and the role of law. He rose quickly through the ranks of English society. An accomplished attorney and lecturer on law, he was an obvious choice for selection to Parliament and membership in Henry VIII's court.

More also knew the texture of family life from direct experience. His first wife died after bearing their four children. More soon remarried. The More home in Chelsea was known for its lively atmosphere. It was a place filled with music, literature, humor, and affection. More's friends, including the great Christian humanist scholar Erasmus, often pointed to More's unselfish love for his wife and the sacrifices he made for her and the children. More once apologized for delivering the manuscript of his book *Utopia* so late to the publisher, explaining that family needs took priority: "When I have return[ed] home, I must talk with my wife, chat with my children and confer with my servants."[3] He was also a model of friendship, as Erasmus noted: "Whoever desires a perfect example of true friendship will seek it nowhere to better purpose than in More."[4]

ROBERT BOLT'S *A Man for All Seasons* gets More right in many ways. Still, the Thomas More of history is much more complex and interesting than any drama will ever show. More was a brilliant lawyer, gifted author, tough political figure, and loving father and husband— but most importantly, he was a person with the courage to say *no*, even when saying *no* meant humiliation and suffering. More was a man of principle guided by a properly formed conscience, who died rather than betray either. And this is the reason More's life is relevant even today.

The modern interest in Thomas More has nothing to do with nostalgia for the sixteenth century. It stems from something else. More offers us a model we yearn for but too often lack in our own daily choices and public leaders. More personifies a life lived with courage and conviction, the same virtues that each of us is called to embrace as citizens and as Catholics. More's humanity is what draws us. He is not a plastic saint. He urgently wanted to live; but not at the cost of selling his soul. Thomas More persuades the modern heart not because he wanted to die for his beliefs, but *because he didn't.* He used all of his skills to avoid martyrdom, but he refused to escape it when the price came down to the integrity of his faith. In More, we see what we all instinctively hunger to believe about ourselves; namely, that we too can choose the joy and freedom that flow from loving something and Someone more than our own lives. In More, we recognize the person we secretly wish we were; the person that God created us to be.

More became the saint God wanted not by dramatic words or gestures. He did it by the simple daily habit of examining his actions in the light of his faith. He fed his conscience with prayer. He submitted himself to the routine of seeking and choosing what his Catholic formation knew to be right. This same path to God is open to anyone who sincerely seeks it. Too often we look at the saints and focus on the end result of their lives. We delude ourselves into imagining that sainthood is exclusive; that holiness involves extraordinary gifts. It isn't. It doesn't. God created all of us to be saints. The only thing that sets a saint like More apart from the rest of us is that he persevered in his pursuit of God's will without excuses or alibis. More's life was never easy. He had many talents, but he worked tirelessly to develop them. The same gifts that made him a great lawyer and statesman also offered him the biggest temptations to serious sin: ambition, greed, the abuse of power and pride.

Through his private life, More teaches us the beauty of family, friendship, and love. In his public life, More teaches us the gravity of politics and the use and misuse of state authority. As an attorney, More naturally had great respect for the law. He revered the role it plays in ordering human affairs with justice and reason. Lawmaking is the people's most serious business and a profoundly moral enterprise. Thus, public service is never legitimately about personal power or influence. It is about shaping society to the right moral principles.

All law, on issues from jaywalking to homicide, is rooted in morality because it codifies what we *ought* to do. *Ought* is a morally loaded word. People make laws to encourage right behavior and discourage wrong behavior, and to coordinate the behavior of all for the sake of the common good. More believed human law is needed to provide basic behavioral boundaries and to protect the relative justice and peace among citizens. He knew that the grim alternative was that "people without law would rush forth into every kind of crime." But at the same time, More was deeply skeptical of human power. He understood that every political system would need to struggle to keep the inevitable human faults of its leaders in check—which is why obedience to proper authority and law was at the heart of More's political vocation.

As the former jurist Robert Bork wrote:

> For More, morality was superior to both human law and the will of the sovereign in that it could be used to shape or to alter that law and that will, though not to justify disobedience to it. This clearly appears in *Utopia,* where he argued that it was a man's duty to enter public life despite the evil necessarily entailed, saying "That which you cannot turn to good, so to order it that it be not very bad." In a word, try to make law as moral as you can, More constantly argued; but when it is made, whatever it commands, morality lies in obedience. If disobedience is ever justified, it is only when the issue is of transcendent importance and when you are absolutely sure of the right and wrong of the matter. In a democratic polity there can be such occasions, but they will be extremely rare.[5]

Unfortunately, we can take the wrong lessons from More, as well as the right ones. Part of his appeal is that we tend to imagine him in our own modern image: the majestic individual set on doing things his way, heroically celebrating disobedience. But if we view More through the lens of twenty-first-century American foibles, we flatter ourselves and cheapen his witness.

More believed he had to follow his conscience, but not because he thought he was smarter or holier than anyone else. He would have quickly seen that for what it is: vanity. More obeyed his conscience because he knew he was obligated to obey God first. And knowing his personal sins and weaknesses, he *also* knew his duty to rightly form his conscience by anchoring it in truth outside his own will. He saw that his Catholic formation of conscience depended on everything the Protestant reformers of his day seemed ready to destroy: authority, tradition, and law. More respected the authority of his king, but he could not accept Henry's claim to supreme spiritual authority because More knew his duty was to a higher law. His sacrifice was not an act of self-assertion. It was the opposite. It was an act of obedience. Only thus do More's last words make sense as he neared the scaffold: "I die the King's good servant, but God's first."

DRAWING TOO SIMPLE a link between Thomas More's life and the issues facing modern U.S. leaders would overstate American problems and understate More's sacrifice. Still, Catholic attorneys and lawmakers often invoke the memory of More for good reason: While candidates don't go to the scaffold in American political life, they can still lose their careers, and they can most certainly lose their integrity. Given the power of the United States, the witness of Thomas More has value for every Catholic public official, today more than ever.

Over the past fifty years, as we've already seen, no one embodies the rise of American Catholic political influence better than John F. Kennedy. His public career was a fork in the road for a generation of Catholics in thinking about the relationship of church and state. In effect, if not deliberately, Kennedy created a model of Catholic political service that sorted personal faith and public service into separate compartments. He did it for understandable reasons: to ease traditional American prejudices about Catholic loyalty to the country. But in hindsight, the cost has been high.

No discord exists between Catholic thought and democratic society when both are properly understood. It's also clear that political integrity or the lack thereof is not party-specific. Historically, most American Catholics preferred the Democratic Party because it generally spoke for Catholic interests better than any other party, at least until abortion emerged as a central national issue. Today Catholic loyalties—assuming a "Catholic" voting bloc even exists—are more complex. Today, in practice, *all* political parties have self-described Catholics who are willing to trade their religious and moral convictions for power. All political parties have parts of their platforms that fly in the face of Catholic teaching. And all political parties contain Catholics who like to keep their personal faith tucked safely away at home. This is why Thomas More has so much to teach us, even today: He always placed the moral content of an issue before factional loyalty and personal interests.

For Catholics, the civil order has its own sphere of responsibility and its own autonomy apart from the church. But that cannot mean that civil authorities are exempt from moral engagement and criticism, either by individual believers or by the church as a body. When the "separation of church and state" that John F. Kennedy tried to articulate in his career starts to mean divorcing religious faith from public life, it soon leads to separating government from morality and citizens from their consciences. And that leads to politics without character, which has now become a national disease.

Given America's thriving religious landscape in 1960, Kennedy could hardly have known where his words on the separation of church and state would lead later generations of Catholic candidates and elected leaders. But two of Kennedy's political heirs—Mario Cuomo and Robert Casey Sr.—interpreted his legacy in different and instructive ways. Both Cuomo and Casey were Democrats. Both were talented. Both were governors. Both were active, practicing Catholics.

Mario Cuomo served as governor of New York from

1983 until 1995. He spent his entire tenure amid the abortion wars that followed *Roe v. Wade.* As a Catholic citizen and politician, Cuomo wrestled with the abortion question. Because he was governor of one of the nation's key states, as well as a man of intellect and legal skill, his answers helped set the tone for the country.

In the midst of a heated 1984 presidential election with abortion as a major issue, Mario Cuomo offered his views in a University of Notre Dame lecture.[6] He took a sympathetic view of the role of religious values in public life. He argued that constitutionally protected political and religious freedoms should apply equally to the most politically active religious believers, as well as to the strongest critics of religious influence in the public square.

Cuomo did not dispute anyone's right to act politically on the basis of his or her religious beliefs. He agreed with the importance of religious values in political debates. Instead, he focused on how those values might best translate into public policy. In effect, he argued that our religious and moral reflection must be balanced by political realities and prudence. He acknowledged that his mission as a Catholic was to further the Gospel in all aspects of his life. But he asked, "Am [I] in conscience required to do everything I can as Governor to translate all my religious values into the laws and regulations of the State of New York or the United States?" His answer was simple. "My church and my conscience require me to believe certain things about divorce, birth control and abortion. My church does not order me—under pain of sin or expulsion—to pursue my salvific mission according to a precisely defined political plan."

Cuomo said that he and his wife accepted Catholic teaching on abortion, seeing it as a moral evil. But he also argued that no clear-cut political program existed to make this moral truth a legislative reality: "The Catholic trying to make moral and prudent judgments in the political realm must discern which, if any, of the actions one could take would be best."

Cuomo concluded that the common good is best served by legalized abortion. He felt that outlawing abortion would be a greater evil. He said that even cutting off state funding for abortion would be unjust.

His logic was straightforward. It tracked back to a Kennedy-inspired sense of the separation of church and state. Cuomo argued that in a diverse society such as America, private morality, especially when based on religion, should never be forced upon others. The same freedom of conscience that would allow someone to accept a particular religious belief should also give someone else the right to reject it. Issues of private morality should be left to individuals to choose for themselves. Cuomo felt the issue of abortion fit this description. As a matter of his own conscience, he would refrain from imposing the Catholic teaching about abortion on non-Catholics.

For critics, the problems with this reasoning were at

least three. First, abortion is not mainly a religious issue but a matter of human rights—in this case, the conceived child's right to life. Second, abortion is never a private matter. It always has social consequences because someone—the unborn child—always dies, often with mental and physical side effects for the mother. Third, the logic of the Cuomo approach breaks down in practice. While Governor Cuomo felt unable to impose his views about abortion on the people of New York, he apparently felt comfortable doing something very similar by vetoing the death penalty twelve different times.

Robert Casey Sr., Pennsylvania's governor from 1987 until 1995, took a different path. Like Cuomo, Casey opposed abortion. Unlike Cuomo, he also worked to protect the unborn child—and therefore against permissive abortion—in his public service. In doing so, he cut against the leaders of his party and experienced the consequences by being publicly snubbed at the 1992 national party convention.

Casey saw his political vocation as one of fighting for the little guy. He found a natural home in the Democratic Party: "I come from a long line of Democrats. My father and grandfather, all the Caseys, were Democrats as far back as the eye can see."[7] He believed that the Democrats had drawn blue-collar workers, like his family, to the party because the Democrats were the party of the poor and forgotten: "It was a party dedicated to defending the weak; to helping the dispossessed; to welcoming the stranger. Let the other parties look to those at the plateaus and summits of life. We would look, in the words of Hubert Humphrey, to those in the shadows of life; those in the twilight of life; and those in the dawn of life."[8]

Casey took great pride in being a Democrat. He believed in his party throughout his life. But he also felt that Democrats could no longer honestly speak for the weak and poor if they refused to reopen their circle of compassion to include the unborn.

In his own University of Notre Dame address in 1995, Casey weighed the results of abortion on demand:

> It was sold to America, this idea, as a kind of social cure, a resolution. Instead, it has left us wounded and divided. We were promised it would broaden the circle of freedom. Instead, it has narrowed the circle of humanity. We were told the whole matter was settled and would soon pass from our minds. Twenty years later, it tears at our souls. And so, it is for me the bitterest of ironies that abortion on demand found refuge, found a home—and it pains me to say this—found a home in the national Democratic Party. My party, the party of the weak, the party of the powerless.
>
> You see, to me, protecting the unborn child fol-

lows naturally from everything I know about my party and about my country. Nothing could be more foreign to the American experience than legalized abortion. It is inconsistent with our national character, with our national purpose, with all that we've done, and with everything we hope to be.[9]

We can best understand Casey's words as a plea to American Catholics at large, regardless of their political party. In his book *Fighting for Life*, Casey leaves us with this message: "Give your country not what it wants or will reward, but what it needs. Lend it in your own lives that goodness without which it cannot be great, and the grace without which it cannot be saved: Press on!"[10]

Governors Casey and Cuomo each had very fruitful careers of public service. Both sought to live their Catholic faith in a serious way. Both pursued what they saw as the common good. Their actions now belong to the public record, and we can esteem the goodwill of both. It's fair though to observe that one man said *no* to the direction of his party, and the other did not. It may also be fair to argue—as many do—that one man gave his party what it needed, and the other, what it wanted.

CATHOLIC POLITICAL LEADERS will always face tensions between their faith and civil duty. They can't be avoided. Thomas More understood that laws are vital to any civilized society. Thus, in the words of More's biographer Gerard Wegemer, More advocated "respect for all laws, even unjust ones. In the face of an unjust law, More advised waiting for a 'place and time convenient' to advocate change."[11] Patience, compromise, and prudence were More's familiar friends. But in the face of serious evil, he knew their limits. He also knew how easily they can mask a deep moral laziness and cowardice. The time and place to press for changing bad laws must eventually come. If not, compromise becomes the casket for a leader's integrity.

More knew that the only way just laws can emerge and be enforced is through citizens with well-formed consciences. Wegemer notes that for More, conscience provides "the metaphysical foundation and the ultimate binding force of law, arising from the very structure of one's being and not merely . . . as the result of threatened punishment."[12] Elected leaders must make laws that reflect a well-formed conscience. When such laws are not produced, those same leaders must press to change them.

The witness of Thomas More remains strong for a reason. God may not call us to be martyrs in blood, but he certainly does call us to be martyrs of the daily kind—the kind who live lives with courage and Catholic conviction; the kind who demand personal integrity and good public policy from our political leaders. Each of us shapes the spirit of our nation. Each of us helps choose the direction our country will take in the future. Citizenship, as More well understood, is serious business. We need to recover the character to say *yes* to what our country needs, *no* to what it doesn't, and the good sense to know the difference.

10.

WHAT NEEDS TO BE DONE

AVERY DULLES, THE AMERICAN Jesuit theologian and cardinal, once wrote that "the greatest danger facing the Church in our country today is that of an excessive and indiscreet accommodation."[1]

I agree. And if we want to know what needs to be done today to best serve our country as Catholics, we can start by admitting that the cultural and political assumptions of the Catholic Church in the United States over the last forty years have largely failed. These failures have weakened the spiritual identity of many Catholics. They have also rendered the American Catholic witness to the Gospel partial and unsure. And they have left our nation without a credible alternative to a way of life that every day seems to grow more remote from the Christian ideal.

This is tall talk, and claims like these need justification. Many would argue that the postwar era has seen huge success for Catholics as they finally arrived in the American mainstream after two hundred years of discrimination. Numbering 69 million today, Catholics make up nearly one-quarter of the total American population.

Economically and socially, Catholics have climbed out of the cultural ghetto and have solidly rooted themselves in the middle and upper-middle classes. By some counts, more than 150 Catholics now serve in Congress, including a quarter of all U.S. senators. A majority of U.S. Supreme Court justices, as I write these words in 2007, are also Catholic.

Yet we can fairly ask: What difference has it made? What impact have these Catholic gains really had on American public life? We can point to many individual successes and examples of forceful Catholic witness. But American culture is not noticeably more ethical or upright. Nor can we argue that America's public square is more informed by the spirit of the Gospel.

Traces of our country's Christian origins remain visible. Americans are broadly a people of faith who value religion, fair play, and common decency. Most Americans are generous and capable of great sacrifices for others, both at home and abroad. Americans have a genuine respect for human rights, freedom, and the rule of law. Catholics share all these traits with their fellow citizens.

Yet there is another America; a kind of dark mirror image of our ideals and self-understanding. This is an America of ethnic and racial injustice, selfishness, consumer greed, and careerism, where popular culture grows increasingly brutish and vulgar. This is an America where half of all marriages end in divorce, where four of every ten children are born out of wedlock, and roughly a million more children are killed each year in the womb. Millions are forgotten and left behind by poverty in this America. Religion is increasingly belittled in the political conversation in this America, and the conversation itself has grown uncivil, indifferent, and unreasoned. Finally, in this America, ordinary citizens show a growing cynicism about the future of our common life together.[2]

Again: What difference do Catholics really make? American bishops have not lacked a civic voice. Since the 1970s, the nation's bishops have offered their moral counsel on issues ranging from civil rights to abortion, to war and peace, to immigration and economic justice.

But the negative trends in American public life have continued. More troubling still are indicators within the church herself.

About one in five U.S. parishes now have no resident priest because of steep declines in priestly numbers and men preparing for the priesthood. In 1965, 49,000 men were studying in Catholic seminaries. In 2006, the number had shrunk to 5,600. Mass attendance has also dropped sharply since the 1960s. Only one in three American Catholics now attends Mass regularly on Sunday. Some observers claim that defections from the Catholic faith have grown so rapidly that the church has become a kind of farm system for other Christian groups.

The truth may be even more unsettling. Many Catholics leave the church not for other religions but for no religion at all. Finally, surveys routinely show that Catholics either don't know basic Catholic teachings or simply don't accept them. And this bears out in their daily behavior. Catholics get divorced, have abortions, and use contraceptives at roughly the same rates as their neighbors.[3]

These problems didn't develop overnight. While some Catholics look back to the 1940s and '50s as a kind of "golden age" for the church in America, the seeds of our difficulty today had already taken root even then. In 1947, Reverend John Hugo, a theologian and retreat leader with Dorothy Day's Catholic Worker movement, described "the spiritual condition of our people" in these strikingly familiar terms:

> It is customary for some to take a rosy view [of American Catholic life] . . . basing their optimism on tables of statistics concerning the growth of the Catholic population, the income and resources of the Church, the number of communions, etc. But such a method of computation is very unreliable where spiritual realities are concerned. Were it of any value, we could compute the degree of religious fervor from the quantities of grease burnt in votive stands, and our optimism would soar to the very skies . . .

[But] even in the case of those who are wholly faithful to the external obligations of religion, there is often little evidence, aside from their devotions, that they are living Christian lives. Large areas of their lives are wholly unilluminated by their faith. Their ideas, their attitudes, their views on current affairs, their pleasure and recreations, their tastes in reading and entertainment, their love of luxury, comfort and bodily ease, their devotion to success, their desire of money, their social snobbishness, racial consciousness, nationalistic narrowness and prejudice, their bourgeois complacency and contempt of the poor: In all these things they are indistinguishable from the huge sickly mass of paganism which surrounds them.[4]

Written sixty years ago, Hugo's words ring even truer today. Catholics have made themselves indistinguishable from their non-Catholic neighbors. They have the same virtues and vices. And this is why the culture isn't more "Catholic" or "Christian," even though Catholics make up 23 percent of the population. A kind of foggy worldliness has settled into the American Catholic soul. In effect, a great many Catholics keep the Catholic brand name, but they freelance what it means.

The point is this: American Catholics now face a crisis of faith, mission, and leadership—and the task of fixing it falls *equally* on Catholic laypeople and their bishops. Too many Catholics, including too many clergy, seem to assume a guaranteed grounding of success, stability, energy, and security for the church in the United States that is arguably eroding right out from under them. In fact, the church in the United States faces very serious questions about her future; questions that lack any easy programmatic answers.[5] What I can offer here, as I've tried to provide throughout these pages, is only one bishop's views drawn from my own pastoral experience. The duty to think and act, however, belongs to all of us—bishops, priests, religious, and laypeople—in different ways.

FOR CATHOLICS, EVERY new beginning must start with a return to Jesus Christ, the Gospel, and the church. The heart of renewal is pretty straightforward: Do we *really* believe that Jesus Christ is our savior? Do we *really* believe that the Gospels are the Word of God? Do we *really* believe that the Catholic Church is the true mother church that Christ himself founded, and that she teaches in his name? Many of us who call ourselves "Catholic" live as if we'd never really thought about any of these questions. In fact, by our actions, many of us witness a kind of practical atheism: paying lip service to God, but living as if he didn't exist. Many of us don't really believe we need a savior. In fact, we don't see anything we need to be *saved from.*

Renewal begins from the inside out. T̶ equally to persons and societies. Every one day, must start again to "repent and believe in ᴛ... Gospel." That means accepting the truth that we need Jesus Christ in our lives—that he is our only salvation; that his Gospel is the only way to live; and that his church is our mother and guide. These interior acts of faith are not empty pieties; when sincere, they will always have external, public consequences. As the epistle says, "We have seen *and testify* that the Father has sent his Son as the Savior of the world" (1 John 4:14; emphasis added).

Renewal means that we must take a hard look at *how* we proclaim and live our Catholic faith in this culture.

Over the last five decades at least, many Catholic leaders, lay and ordained alike, have been guided by two assumptions. The first is that the church can go a long way toward carrying out her mission by taking part like other interested parties in America's democratic process; by making statements, issuing policy analyses, building alliances, and lobbying lawmakers. The second assumption is really more like a temperament. American Catholic leaders have cultivated a chronic optimism about the compatibility of American culture with Catholic faith and values.

In principle, these are sound assumptions. Catholics from Charles Carroll to the late Cardinal John O'Connor of New York, a former navy chaplain, have loved this country and revered its democratic institutions. But we always need to compare our assumptions to the real terrain of American life. As Catholics, we need to take a much tougher and more self-critical look at ourselves as believers; at the issues underlying today's erosion of Catholic identity; and at the wholesale assimilation—*absorption* might be a better word—of Catholics by American culture.

Too many Catholics have unconsciously come to see the church through the lens of American secular politics; to falsely divide the "institutional" church from an imaginary "real" church. Too many Catholics use the church as an arena in which interest-group battles are fought out while organizing lobbies and pressure blocs, demonizing ideological opponents, and interpreting relationships largely in terms of power. None of this has anything to do with Catholic ecclesiology, and it's a temptation that infects nearly all parties in the church, no matter what their point of departure—left or right. This may be the most distressing example of how assimilation to American culture has produced distortions in Catholic life, of which we're only dimly aware and that now require a huge effort of reevangelization.

Meanwhile, we need to be clear about what the separation of church and state really means, and what it *doesn't* mean. We need to remember how—and, more importantly, *why*—this doctrine took shape the way it has. The modern secular interpretation of church-state separation doctrine has explicitly anti-Catholic roots in the nineteenth century. And this is no partisan Catholic claim. It's the judgment of leading independent historians and legal scholars like Daniel Dreisbach, Philip Hamburger, John McGreevy, and others.[6] In recent years, a majority opinion of the Supreme Court has even acknowledged it.

Key Supreme Court decisions in the 1940s and '50s were shaped by a perverse anxiety then common in American intellectual circles about "Catholic power." Scholars have identified anti-Catholic code language and assumptions in these decisions, notably in Justice Hugo Black's opinions. Black, of course, was a former Ku Klux Klansman notorious for his lifelong hostility toward the Catholic Church. But on the high court he was not alone in his prejudice.

The long history and "shameful pedigree" of the Court's anti-Catholicism was reckoned by Justice Clarence Thomas in his majority opinion in *Mitchell v. Helms* (2000), a case involving public aid for religious schools:

> Hostility to aid to pervasively sectarian schools has a shameful pedigree that we do not hesitate to disavow . . . Opposition to aid to "sectarian" schools acquired prominence in the 1870s with Congress' consideration (and near passage) of the Blaine Amendment, which would have amended the Constitution to bar any aid to sectarian institu-

tions. Consideration of the amendment arose at a time of pervasive hostility to the Catholic Church and to Catholics in general, and it was an open secret that "sectarian" was code for "Catholic." Notwithstanding its history, of course, "sectarian" could, on its face, describe the school of any religious sect, but the Court eliminated this possibility of confusion when, in *Hunt v. McNair,* it coined the term "pervasively sectarian"—a term which, at that time, could be applied almost exclusively to Catholic parochial schools . . . In short, nothing in the Establishment Clause requires the exclusion of pervasively sectarian schools from otherwise permissible aid programs, and other doctrines of this Court bar it. *This doctrine, born of bigotry,* should be buried now.[7]

What history shows us is that the American political and legal process, for all its strengths, has rarely been neutral toward the Catholic Church. Modern separation doctrine was not born of a dispassionate search for the common good. It grew directly out of bigotry. It began in a bald effort to wall Catholics out of the nation's public life.

The intentions of America's founders have often been twisted out of shape by this anti-Catholic bigotry. The irony is that, in our own day, policies once aimed against Catholics have blown back on everyone else. Now *all* re-

ligious believers, not just committed Catholics, are su.
pect and risk exclusion from the public square.

Catholics—and I mean all of us, bishops and laypeople alike—need to admit that we've been too naive, too
often, in our past political assumptions. American Catholics have taken part in good faith in a system that sometimes operates in bad faith. The Protestant theologian
Stanley Hauerwas once warned that the great weakness of
Christian witness in our time is that we preach as though
we don't have enemies. But we do. In our legitimate
hopes for a role in American life, Catholics have ignored
an unpleasant truth: that there are active, motivated
groups in modern American society that bitterly resent
the Catholic Church and the Christian Gospel, and would
like to silence both.

Many Catholics since Vatican II have recoiled almost
instinctively from traditional images of the "church mil-
itant." But like it or not, that is exactly what we are—or
should be. We are in a struggle for the souls of our people and our country. We ignore this at our own peril. We
also fail as disciples.

"THE GREATEST FAILURE in leadership is for the
leader to be afraid to speak and act as a leader," the Viet-
namese archbishop (later cardinal) F. X. Nguyen Van
Thuan once said.[8] Van Thuan had been a bishop only a
year when Saigon fell to the communists in 1975. The

new regime locked him in forced-labor camps and prisons for thirteen years. He spent the last nine in solitary confinement, in a vermin-infested cell with no windows. Yet he was a leader even in his captivity. Under pain of death, he celebrated the Eucharist with bread and wine smuggled in to him. He wrote words of encouragement and hope that he smuggled out to his people.

American Catholics face none of the direct persecution that so many Christians around the world routinely endure. We might be more alive if we did. Instead, we're weighed down by distraction, indifference, and comfort; by all the moral narcotics that come with an open and materially abundant society.

It's an old problem. It comes whenever the Church and her people begin to get too comfortable as part of society's structures. Saint Hilary, bishop of Poitiers, wrote about it in the fourth century:

> But today we fight an insidious persecutor, an enemy who flatters . . . He does not stab us in the back but fills our stomachs. He does not seize our property and thereby give us life. He stuffs our pockets to lead us to death. He does not cast us into dungeons thereby setting us on the path to freedom. He imprisons us in the honors of the palace. He showers priests with honors, so that there will be no good bishops. He builds churches that he may destroy the faith.[9]

As American Catholics, most of us have food to eat and work that puts cash in our pockets. We have money to build churches, access to lawmakers, and talented, influential people in our communities. Our achievements and hard work give us a unique power to bear witness to the Gospel. But we often face enormous counterpressures to stay silent; to compromise on matters of justice; to go along with fashionable opinion. And this is just as true for bishops and other clergy as it is for Catholics at every level of public life.

We can take a lesson from the early church. The emperor Valens ruled the eastern half of the Roman Empire in the AD 360s. He was a brutal man at a time of bitter political and religious turmoil, and he sought to destroy the orthodox faith in Christ. Saint Basil the Great, then the bishop of Caesarea, confronted him face-to-face about his policies. "Never has anyone dared to speak to me with such freedom," Valens said. Basil replied, "Obviously you have never met a bishop before."[10]

This is how Christ calls bishops to lead: with candor, simplicity, and courage. In every situation, men and women must know that they have "met a bishop." Not a privileged dignitary, not a corporate executive; but a leader and teacher, a true apostle of Jesus Christ.

Something similar is true for every lay Catholic. People should come away from every encounter with every American Catholic knowing that they have met a true *Catholic*. Cardinal Van Thuan's call for courage in Catholic leaders applies to laypeople as forcefully as it does to clergy—and in some ways, more so. Renewal happens from the inside out. Priests are poor substitutes for the lay vocation when it comes to working in the public square. If the secular world is to be redeemed, it must happen *from the inside out*, which means the task belongs primarily to faithful, well-informed, committed Catholic laypeople.

People, not words, make converts. This is because the Catholic faith is much more than a set of principles we agree to, but rather an entirely new way of life. *People must see that new life being lived.* They must see the joy that it brings. They must see the union of the believer with Jesus Christ.

The Gospel spreads by personal contact and friendship. But true friendship never survives long with disingenuousness, or by leaving vital Christian truths and opinions unspoken. Obviously, we should always respect the freedom of others. We need to preach love *with* love. We need to know our world; we need to find the words and actions that will persuade others by reason and example. But we also need the courage to preach the Gospel in season and out, even when we know our message will not be popular. Again, to quote Hilary, the ancient bishop of Poitiers: "Further silence is not a sign of discretion, but of little faith."[11]

Too often in recent decades, we American Catholics—both clergy and lay—have made ourselves guilty of "kneeling before the world," in Jacques Maritain's famous words. We find ourselves softening the Christian message—the cross, the call to holiness, the reality that all men and women are under the judgment of God—because these truths aren't considered respectful in a secularized, pluralistic society.

One pervasive form of this genuflection to the world is a pragmatic "reductionism" in offering the Gospel. To gain a public hearing, many Catholics find themselves justifying the church's social teachings in practical, *humanitarian* terms.

Pope John Paul II knew this kind of false compromise very well: "The temptation today is to reduce Christianity to merely human wisdom, a pseudo-science of well-being. In our heavily secularized world a 'gradual secularization of salvation' has taken place, so that people strive for the good of man, but man who is truncated, reduced to his merely horizontal dimension."[12]

Here, most especially, all of us who are Catholic need to examine our consciences. We can never allow ourselves to offer an abridged version of the Gospel. We can never let Catholic social doctrine become an end in itself. The Catholic faith is much more than just another public philosophy or useful set of social programs. The church is not an association of social workers. She is a community of believers and disciples. In fact, the church's social service has no meaning outside her Christ-centered faith.

Catholic social teaching reveals the destiny of the human person and the purpose of human community. It preaches personal and communal action to bring about the real transformation of society. This is *revolutionary* in the truest sense. It eclipses Karl Marx and every other modern false prophet. We need to make the Gospel's social dimension a powerful part of our own and other people's lives. And we need to restore a commitment to truly *Catholic* action in the political process, in our party politics, in our voting, and also in our political leadership. We need to understand once again that holding public office is not simply a useful service to society, but a *magnanimous and morally noble* vocation—and why.

Catholic social doctrine is the concrete public expression of the Gospel. Saint John's question remains real: How can we love God whom we *can't* see, if we don't love our brothers and sisters whom we *do* see? (1 John 4:20). The following words of Pope Benedict XVI should inspire and at the same time admonish us:

> If I have no contact whatsoever with God in my life, then I cannot see in the other [person] anything more than the other, and I am incapable of seeing in him the image of God. But if in my life I fail completely to heed others, solely out of a desire to be "devout" and to perform my "religious duties," then my relationship with God will also grow arid. It becomes merely "proper," but love-

less. Only my readiness to encounter my neigh
and to show him love makes me sensitive to C
as well. Only if I serve my neighbor can my ey
be opened to what God does for me and how much
he loves me . . . Love of God and love of neighbor
are thus inseparable, they form a single commandment. But both live from the love of God who has
loved us first. No longer is it a question, then, of a
"commandment" imposed from without and calling for the impossible, but rather of a freely-
bestowed experience of love from within, a love
which by its very nature must then be shared with
others. Love grows through love.[13]

We need to root the social dimension of our Catholic
faith, and everything else we do, in God's love, which is
the fuel for our mission of evangelization. We can't offer
Catholic social action to the men and women of the
world without at the same time offering them Jesus
Christ. Pope John Paul II reminded us that Catholic social doctrine, at its root, is *missionary.* It is *"an instrument
of evangelization.* As such it proclaims God in his mystery
of salvation in Christ to every human being . . . In this
light, *and only in this light,* does it concern itself with
everything else . . . the ordering of national and international society, economic life, culture, war and peace, and
respect for life."[14]

The Catholic Church exists to make Jesus Christ known; to bring the will of men and women into alignment with God's will through a relationship with Jesus Christ, the Son of God. The church has a vital role in building peace and reconciliation, promoting justice, and defending creation. But she does that first by proclaiming "the whole counsel of God" (Acts 20:27). Without God, no matter how good our intentions, all our humanitarian ambitions eventually drift toward tyranny, because as Charles Péguy once said, tyranny is always better organized than freedom.

The church serves her humanitarian mission best by doing what Christ founded her to do: to make saints. If we Catholics hope to transform America and not simply be digested by it, we need to raise up a new kind of genius, a generation of saints, through our prayer and zeal, through our personal witness, through our faithful devotion to the sacraments. These things matter *profoundly*. They are not the "religious icing" on the substance of the Christian message—they are the soul of it; the cornerstones of a truly Catholic life. The final lines of Léon Bloy's classic novel, *The Woman Who Was Poor*, should burn in the heart of every serious believer: "There is only one misery and that is—*not to be saints.*" This is exactly the fire we need to set ablaze in our own lives and in the lives of Catholics across the United States.

·   ·   ·

CHRIST SAID HE came to cast fire upon the earth (Luke 12:49). He meant the holy fire—the fire of charity—of men and women in love with God and zealous to bring that love to their neighbors and their nation. This has always been the secret of Christian history. Every vocation, lay, religious, or clergy, is a form of mission. The choices of one person, made for the love of God, can transform the lives of many others. The conscious choice to *repent and believe the Gospel* is the most radical decision a human being can make.

The first Christians practiced what they said they believed. They didn't need an elaborate program. They lived their faith, and it had radical consequences. They could no longer go on thinking or behaving like their neighbors. Their faith grew contagious. It spread soul to soul like wildfire. People wanted a share of the love that animated these first believers. And within four hundred years, the world was a different place. A new civilization, a Christian civilization, had been born.

The Gospel still has that power today—if we preach it and live it; if we make the choice for Christ in everything we do. Amid the anticlerical persecutions in revolutionary France, Reverend Jean Baptiste Henri Lacordaire, said, "A man cannot dictate events, but he can always preserve right principles in his heart." This is true for all of us; for every American Catholic citizen. We need to preserve the faith in our hearts and live it fully with our lives. God will do the rest. But we need to do our part.

In one of their early confrontations, King Henry VIII taunted Bishop John Fisher, the great bishop-martyr of the English Reformation who remained faithful to Rome and opposed Henry's marriage to Anne Boleyn, with this remark: "Well, well, it shall make no matter . . . for you are but one man." Catholics face the world's same taunting today: the temptation to think that society is too far gone, that our problems are too complex for any of us to make a difference. But one person can always make a difference—*if* that person believes in Jesus Christ and seeks to do his will. We're not called to get results. We're called to be faithful.

Thomas More is better remembered than John Fisher, though both men, who were friends, showed the same heroic courage and died for the same reasons under the same English king. Still, this imbalance is fair, because laypeople have the task of infusing a nation's laws, structures, and culture with a truly Christian spirit. Clergy play the *supporting* role: to form men and women for their Christian work of transforming the world. The friendship and mutual witness of Thomas More and John Fisher make them the ideal model for Catholics today.

Fisher always kept an image of John the Baptist on the altar of his private chapel. And he died in a fashion similar to John—beheaded for refusing to allow the truth of the Gospel to be twisted to the whims of a selfish king. He died like John because he lived like him: proclaiming Christ and faithful to what he believed, though almost everyone around him had grown afraid. This lesson is as old as Christianity. Pope Liberius, one of the first bishops of Rome to be hauled before a hostile emperor, said it best: "The truth of the faith is not lessened by the fact that I stand alone."

What needs to be done by Catholics today for their country? The answer is: *Don't lie.* If we say we're Catholic, we need to prove it. America's public life needs people willing to stand alone, without apologies, for the truth of the Catholic faith and the common human values it defends. One person can make a difference—if that individual has a faith he or she is willing to suffer for; a faith that can say, as Fisher did in greeting his executioner, "I come to die for the faith of Christ and Christ's Catholic Church."

11.

FAITHFUL CITIZENS

AFTER SOME TIME SPENT living abroad, the writer David Brooks came home to the United States in the 1990s. He soon noticed that "most people, at least among the college educated set, seemed to have rebel attitudes and social-climbing attitudes all scrambled together." These highly educated folks seemed to "have one foot in the bohemian world of creativity and another in the bourgeois realm of ambition and worldly success." He named this new establishment "the Bobos," or bourgeois bohemians—an upper-middle-class meritocracy grounded in both the countercultural 1960s and greedy 1980s, and determined to have it both ways. He observed that "in America today, it's genius and geniality that enable you to join the elect."[1]

As an author, Brooks has rare talent, and the Bobo values he describes bear some thought. Bobos *like* flexidoxy, a cocktail of religious flexibility and tradition gently stirred. "They treasure religion," Brooks notes, "so long as it is conducted in a spirit of moderation rather than zeal."[2] They believe not so much in a Last Judgment as in a Last Discussion.

Bobos *dislike* "podium-pounding 'conviction politicians' of the sort that thrived during the age of confrontation. Instead, they weave together different approaches. They triangulate. They reconcile. They know they have to appeal to diverse groups. They seek a Third Way beyond the old categories of left and right. They march under reconciling banners such as compassionate conservatism, practical idealism, sustainable development, smart growth, prosperity with a purpose."[3] The reason they do this is that the two very different decades in which they root themselves—the 1960s and the 1980s—actually shared two basic principles: individualism and freedom. Having won power, the Bobos now find themselves stuck with the fruits of their victory: excessive individualism and excessive freedom. Thus, now that they're running things, Bobos seek to "preserve order and stability and restore community control."[4]

A skeptic might see this as routine class self-interest; or even worse, proof of getting old. Nonetheless, learned wisdom is a beautiful thing. And Brooks argued that by the late 1990s, Bobo maturity had created a time of relative American peace, prosperity, and centrism. On the surface, it wasn't a bad achievement. But it hid a couple of problems.

The first problem is this: The world tends to drive a

gas-guzzling Humvee over our national complacency. Brooks published *Bobos in Paradise* in 2000. A great deal has changed since. The world has seen 9/11, the spread of extremist Islam, and terror bombings in Europe and Asia. We've had wars in Afghanistan and Iraq, saber-rattling by Iran and North Korea, and a bitter American immigration crisis with deep human and economic implications. As Brooks worried in his book, "In preferring politicians who are soggy sympathizers and in withdrawing from great national and ideological disputes for the sake of local and community pragmatism, we may be losing touch with the soaring ideals and high ambitions that have always separated America from other nations."[5]

He added that "we may become a nation that enjoys the comforts of private and local life but has lost any sense of national union and any sense of a unique historical mission. The fear is that America will decline not because it overstretches, but because it enervates as its leading citizens decide that the pleasures of an oversized kitchen are more satisfying than the conflicts and challenges of patriotic service."[6]

The second Bobo problem is more believer-specific. Somebody famous once said, "Man shall not live by bread alone but by every word that proceeds from the mouth of God" (Matthew 4:4). This is a bit extreme for Bobo taste, which dwells, as Brooks notes, in the moral temperate zone. And yet the Bible that most of us say we believe tells us that the lukewarm will be spit out of Christ's mouth (Revelation 3:16).

SCRIPTURE OUTLINES CHRISTIAN attitudes toward the state in a few key passages. None is better known than this one:

> Then the Pharisees went and took counsel how to entangle him in his talk. And they sent their disciples to him, along with the Herodians, saying "Teacher, we know that you are true, and teach the way of God truthfully, and care for no man; for you do not regard the position of men. Tell us, then, what you think. Is it lawful to pay taxes to Caesar, or not?" But Jesus, aware of their malice, said, "Why put me to the test, you hypocrites? Show me the money for the tax." And they brought him a coin. And Jesus said to them, "Whose likeness and inscription is this?" They said, "Caesar's." Then he said to them, "Render therefore to Caesar the things that are Caesar's, and to God the things that are God's." (Matthew 22:15–21)

We need some background to understand Christ's words. The Caesar on the coin was Tiberius. He was the adopted son of Octavian (Augustus Caesar), who himself had been adopted by Gaius Julius Caesar. In Jesus' lifetime, Caesar was still a family name. It did not become an imperial title until some thirty years after Christ's crucifixion. Jesus lived during the Roman Principate, the early years of the empire. Memories of the Roman Republic still endured. Tiberius was, at least in theory, merely the First Citizen (*princeps*) among equals, not the autocrat of later centuries. Nonetheless, Roman religious and political life mixed deeply, and the gods were used to reinforce state authority. Worshipping the *genius* (essence or spirit) of the emperor had already started under Augustus. The Jews saw this as idolatry. Rome exempted them from the practice. Instead, the Jerusalem Temple offered sacrifices twice a day for Caesar and the Roman nation. But the Jews also resented the emperor's image on military standards and coins. They saw it partly as a form of idol worship but also as a token of their subjection by pagan foreigners.

The Roman presence divided the Jewish people. The word *Pharisee* likely comes from the Aramaic *perishaya* or the Hebrew *perushim*, meaning "the separated." Mainly lay scholars known for interpreting the Torah, the Pharisees were devoted to the synagogue and rigorous in their piety. They opposed the Sadducees, the priestly class from Jerusalem's great families, who dominated the city's leadership and worked comfortably with the Romans.

They also clashed with the Herodians, backers of King Herod and his dynasty, whom many Jews despised as irreligious Roman puppets. Thus the picture of Pharisees and Herodians working together in this Gospel passage is very unusual. Their motive was simple, though. They both hated Jesus. The Pharisees saw Christ as a preacher of heresy, laxity, and blasphemy. The Herodians saw him as a political troublemaker. Either way, he posed a problem.

In the Gospel passage, Christ's enemies reveal themselves in their flattery. They're insincere. They use the words *true* and *truthfully* but abuse them by their duplicity. In fact, they sound curiously like some of the voices today who want to push religion out of politics and God out of the public square—ostensibly for everyone's freedom of conscience; but often because of a particular contempt for Christianity and a distrust for serious faith in general. Jesus names this for what it is: malice and hypocrisy. He sees their purpose. If he supports paying the tax, he can be cast as a Roman collaborator. If he argues against paying the tax, he can be cast as an anti-Roman agitator. We should notice that Jesus doesn't have one of the hated coins, but his enemies do. And while his enemies mention God, they seem much more concerned about Caesar.

Jesus asks whose image and inscription are stamped on the metal. The answer is Caesar. So Christ tells them to give the coin to the ruler who marked it as his own. It's a clever answer. It's also profound. Jesus does three vital things here. First, he acknowledges that Caesar has rights; that a difference does exist between the things that belong to God and the things that belong to Caesar. But second, he desacralizes—in effect, he *demotes*—Caesar by suggesting that Caesar has no rights over those things that belong to God. Only God is God, which means Caesar is *not* God. Caesar's authority has limits. And third, Jesus stays silent about what exactly belongs to either one. Figuring that out belongs to us.

It can be hard work. No detailed map exists because while human nature doesn't change, human circumstances change all the time. Over the centuries, some Christians have used this passage to avoid politics altogether, fearing the taint of "principalities and powers." Caesar is usually happy to agree: The less trouble from believers, the better for him. A certain kind of modern Pharisee sees the Catholic confusion since Vatican II as punishment for the church's efforts at reform and her opening to the goodness in the world. But in fact, cooperation with proper worldly authority is hardwired into Christian thought by both Scripture and Tradition. Christians continued to preach respect for state authority even after Rome crucified their Messiah. Paul's Letter to the Romans reminds Christians, "Let every person be subject to the governing authorities. For there is no authority except from God, and those that exist have been instituted by God. Therefore he who resists the authorities, resists what God has appointed, and those who resist will incur judgment" (Paul 13:1–2).

Note that this is a call for proper obedience, not mindless submission. The key line in these verses from Paul's letter is *"For there is no authority except from God, and those that exist have been instituted by God."* Christians obey secular rulers not because of anything inherent to the rulers. Rather, when rulers properly use their power, they draw their authority from God.

Nonetheless, the eagerness of self-described religious people to abase themselves before Caesar started early. And it continues in the Herodians of our own day. In Luke 23:2, the chief priests and scribes bring Jesus before Pilate and immediately "accuse him, saying, 'We found this man perverting our nation and forbidding us to give tribute to Caesar and saying that he himself is Christ a king.' " In John 19:15, the priests cry out, "We have no king but Caesar." And in Acts 17:6–7, the mob tells the city authorities, "These men, [Paul and Silas] who have turned the world upside down, have come here also, and Jason has received them; and they are all acting against the decrees of Caesar, saying that there is another king, Jesus." For a people so hostile to the worship of rulers, this is odd behavior.

A story from before the birth of Jesus makes the point here. The hedonist philosopher Aristippus once asked a favor from Dionysius, the tyrant of Syracuse. The tyrant refused. Aristippus then wept and pleaded and finally flung himself at the tyrant's feet until he got what he begged for. Later, friends berated him for humbling himself at the ruler's feet. Aristippus answered, "But that's where the tyrant's ears are."

Power can have a miraculous effect on the self-esteem of the person who wields it. It's an equal-opportunity drug. It can work its magic on tyrants, Caesars, and democratically elected public officials. Today's Herodians are better dressed, better fed, better educated, and usually have better public relations counsel, but their message really hasn't changed much. In their mistreatment of the innocent—beginning with the unborn child—they tell us they must deal in the politics of realism; that this is the way of the world. And in a sense, they're right. But the task of the Christian is to change that.

THE ROMAN STATESMAN Cicero once said that "nothing can be useful if it is not at the same time morally good." It's another way of saying that the end never justifies the means. Our goals may be admirable, but if we use bad methods to achieve them, we undermine both our goals and our own moral judgment. What this means for American public life should be obvious. Politics is the art of the possible. Catholics should be realistic and flexible in their political attitudes. But a hierarchy of truths about human behavior exists, and it needs

to guide our decision making. Some things have more
moral weight than others. We all instinctively know this.
Cheating on a test is bad. Embezzling from our employer
is worse. Murdering our neighbor is worst.

Understanding the moral differences among social
issues is crucial. Not all evil things can or should be illegal.[7] Not all issues have the same gravity. A healthy culture can tolerate some forms of evil in the interests of
social peace. Nonetheless, some acts are so evil that tolerating them *itself* becomes a poison that weakens the
whole of society. Civil rights were the key moral issue of
a previous generation. Historically, most African Americans trace their roots in this country to slavery, and slaves
did not have the status of human persons under the law.
The work for racial justice was vital. It remains so today.
But civil rights flow from an even more basic human
right: the right to life.

In our day, sanctity-of-life issues are foundational—
not because of anyone's "religious" views about abortion,
although these are important; but because the act of de-
humanizing and killing the unborn child attacks human
dignity in a uniquely grave way. Deliberately killing the
innocent is *always*, inexcusably wrong. It sets a pattern of
contempt for every other aspect of human dignity. In redefining when human life begins and what is and isn't a
human person, the logic behind permissive abortion
makes all human rights politically contingent.

Vatican II assumed that Catholic citizens would

serve the common good by rooting their actions in a well-formed, comprehensive, mature Catholic sense of social justice. In the United States, this has failed for various reasons. As we've already seen, American Catholic laypeople have earned great economic and educational success. They often serve the public with great skill. But their grasp of their own Catholic faith is often poor or is shaped by an unfriendly wider culture. In the way they actually *apply* their faith, too many American Catholics ignore what they claim—as Catholics—to believe as true.

The indifference, institutionalism, and lack of courage among some bishops that led to the 2002 national sex-abuse crisis are the easiest factors to blame for the erosion of lay confidence in the church. But they are by no means the only factors or even the deepest. History is a long story. The Catholic Church has suffered even uglier failures from her shepherds in the past. The task of bishops is to seek holiness themselves and to lead their people to that same holiness. That means they must *know* their people; truly *love* their people; and speak the truth with clarity and courage.

One of the biggest ironies since the Second Vatican Council is this: Vatican II sought to decentralize Roman authority and restore a wholesome collegiality among bishops. This was a good thing. The Catholic Church is a unique kind of community; neither a dictatorship nor a democracy nor a monolith. She more closely resembles a confederation of families than a multinational corporation. But collegial reform can lead down unintended roads, including a collective approach to responsibility that can be slow, bureaucratic, and overshadow the individual bishop's duty to teach and lead. National statements by the American bishops have often given good guidance to the faithful on issues ranging from economic justice to immigration reform. But the church has no special claim to policy competence. Her task is offering basic principles for her people to apply in daily life. The more specific and complex her statements grow, the more they invite criticism and the more prone they become to charges of partisan bias.

After the 2006 elections, various bishops and lay leaders complained that the periodic *Faithful Citizenship* guide to political issues published by the American bishops was too complex. In their view, the document sorted through too many different issues in a way that left the average Catholic unable to distinguish really pivotal issues from others that were important but not foundational.

The criticism is not entirely fair, and *Faithful Citizenship* was notably revised and improved by America's bishops in 2007. But bishops do need to give clear Catholic teaching to their people. People need to understand the natural hierarchy of truth that exists not just in Christian thought but in daily life. This was exactly why the late Bishop James McHugh, the late Cardinal John O'Connor, and others pressed so often and so long for a pastoral letter like the 1998 bishops' statement, *Living the Gospel of Life*. Based on John Paul II's encyclical *Evangelium Vitae* (The Gospel of Life), *Living the Gospel of Life* restated briefly and clearly the principles that govern Catholic social thought. The heart of that document, paragraph 23, is worth revisiting because it has often been overlooked or overshadowed by other statements:

> Adopting a consistent ethic of life, the Catholic Church promotes a broad spectrum of issues . . . Opposition to abortion and euthanasia does not excuse indifference to those who suffer from poverty, violence and injustice. Any politics of human life must work to resist the violence of war and scandal of capital punishment. Any politics of human dignity must seriously address issues of racism, poverty, hunger, employment, education, housing and health care. Therefore, Catholics should eagerly involve themselves as advocates for the weak and marginalized in all those areas. Catholic public officials are obliged to address each of these issues as they seek to build consistent policies which promote respect for the human person at all stages. *But being "right" in such matters can never excuse a wrong choice regarding direct attacks on innocent human life* [emphasis in original]. Indeed, the failure to protect and defend life in its most

vulnerable stages renders suspect any claims to the "rightness" of positions in other matters affecting the poorest and least powerful of the human community. If we understand the human person as "the temple of the Holy Spirit"—the living house of God—then these latter issues fall logically into place as the crossbeams and walls of that house. *All direct attacks on innocent human life, such as abortion and euthanasia, strike at the house's foundation* [emphasis in original]. These directly and immediately violate the human person's most fundamental right—the right to life. Neglect of these issues is the equivalent of building our house on sand. Such attacks cannot help but lull the social conscience in ways ultimately destructive of other human rights.[8]

In offering his own thoughts on Catholic social teaching, the late Cardinal Joseph Bernardin warned against the misuse of his "seamless garment" imagery to falsely invest different social issues with the same moral gravity. Many social issues are important. Many require our attention. But some issues have more weight than others. Deliberately killing innocent human life, or standing by and allowing it, dwarfs all other social issues. Trying to avoid this fact by redefining when human personhood begins is simply a corrupt and *corrupting* form of verbal gymnastics. And this habit is not the special reserve of our political leaders. The challenge to American bishops as teachers is most forcefully shown by the mail many of us receive from our people in the pews. Quite a few American Catholics feel comfortable in the role of lions when they lecture the church to keep silent about immigration reform or abortion. But they turn into kittens when it comes to demanding a real change of direction from their own political parties and leaders on the very same issues. Persons who claim to be Catholic under such circumstances are deluding themselves. They want the eternity insurance of faith but refuse to pay the premium it involves.

This is a long way from what real Catholic citizenship requires. The words of Ignatius of Antioch, the early bishop and martyr, are worth remembering. He said, "Our task is not one of producing persuasive propaganda. Christianity shows its greatness when it is hated by the world." He also said, "Just beg for me the courage and endurance not only to speak but also to will what is right, so that I may not only be called a Christian, but prove to be one."

A YOUNG WOMAN once told me that she had dated several loyal men, but she was holding out for a faithful one. She made the right choice. Loyalty and fidelity are similar virtues, but they are not the same thing. The root of *loyalty* is the French word *loi* (law). The root of *fidelity* is the Latin word *fides* (trust). Loyalty is ordered to duty. Fidelity is ordered to love. And real love, as every mature adult knows, is both beautiful and demanding. It has nothing to do with indulging or accommodating evil in the person or thing that is loved. Thus, *loving* our country implies a lot more than following the public opinion herd, or muffling our Catholic convictions about right and wrong and the defense of human dignity in the interests of social etiquette.

Writing in the spring of 2007, David Brooks (of Bobo fame) turned his eye on American Catholics.[9] He noted that in social standing and personal wealth, Catholics in the United States had "erased the gap that used to separate them from mainline Protestants." They did this by finding a "quasi-religious sweet spot." In other words, in assimilating, Catholics tended to retain their broad communal heritage but ignore inconvenient Catholic teaching. As a result, American Catholics had created a uniquely productive hybrid culture: a familiar Bobo blend of more or less regular religious practice and more or less regular dissent.

The lessons of this quasi-religious creed, Brooks suggested, are two: First, "if you really wanted to supercharge the nation, you'd fill it with college students who constantly attend church, but who are skeptical of everything they hear there"; and second, always try to be "the least believing member of one of the more observant sects."

This used to be called pragmatism, and pragmatism often works. It's lucrative, and it gets results—if the goals are material and short term. But American political life, though very practical, depends on ideas and beliefs that are large and *long* term; that are *not* built low to the ground; that need a citizenry with right moral character in order to "work." A republic of self-absorbed compromisers with Volvos and good alibis is probably not what the founders had in mind when they gambled their lives on the Revolution. And Americans have always chosen to be better than that in a crisis. Catholics need to remember that now. They need to remember, borrowing from the second century's *Letter to Diognetus*, that "the Christian is to the world what the soul is to the body . . . It is by the soul, enclosed within the body, that the body is held together." Catholics must sustain and give life to the nation in the same way, through their active Christian witness. "Such is the Christian's lofty and divinely appointed function, *from which he is not permitted to excuse himself*" (emphasis added).

The argument that pursuing our Catholic beliefs vigorously in public affairs could lead to a fundamentalist theocracy or a Christian Taliban is dishonest at its root. For one thing, it's *bad history.* As the philosopher Rémi Brague puts it, the two world religions

with a "political" dimension did not acquire it in the same way. Christianity gained ground in the ancient world against the political power of the Roman Empire, which had persecuted Christians for almost three centuries before itself adopting the Christian religion. Islam, after a brief period of trials, triumphed during the lifetime of its founder. It then conquered, by warfare, the right to operate in peace, and even the right to dictate conditions of survival to the adepts of other religions "of the Book." In modern terms we might say that *Christianity conquered the state through civil society; Islam, to the contrary, conquered civil society through the state.* [emphasis in original][10]

In fact, Brague says, "from the start Christianity set itself outside the political domain, and its founding texts bear witness to a distrust of things political."[11]

Christianity was seen as politically subversive precisely because it *denied* the identification of religion and state; God and Caesar. Christian faith did indeed have "political" consequences, but only because it created a new kind of dynamic social organism: the church. For the first time in history, a community was founded not on territory, or the sovereign, or blood or the law, but on a unifying faith that owed its final allegiance to no earthly king. Moreover, Christian faith rooted itself not in a set of ideas but in a person: the person of Jesus Christ, who alone had the right to be called *Kyrios* (Lord). Early Christian martyrs went to their death singing *Deus major est, non Imperatores* (God is the greater One, not the emperors).[12] And this spirit is just as offensive to worldly authority today as it was twenty centuries ago.

Christoph Schönborn, Vienna's cardinal archbishop, once wrote that "Christianity from its early days, and again and again throughout its entire history, became a source of conflict in society." Why? The reason is this: "If Christians merely looked on this world as a waiting room in which one watched for the signal to depart for the heavenly Jerusalem, there would be no cause to think of them as anything more than mere mixed up dreamers. Jesus Christ, however, left behind quite a different charge from that of an inactive waiting around."[13] Instead, Jesus very clearly said, "All authority on heaven and *on earth* has been given to me," and then sent his disciples out to convert the world and to lead all peoples to accept and live his teachings. This Christian mission need not violate the autonomy of the secular order; but it can certainly bruise its vanity.

Joseph Ratzinger, now Pope Benedict XVI, put it this way:

> [The] political task is not the immediate competence of the Church. Respect for a healthy secularity—including the pluralism of political opinions—is essential in the authentic Christian tradition. If the Church were to start transforming

herself into a directly political subject, she would
do less, not more, for the poor and for justice, because she would lose her independence and her
moral authority, identifying herself with a single
political path and with debatable partisan positions. The Church is the advocate of justice and of
the poor precisely because she does not identify
with politicians, nor with partisan interests. Only
by remaining independent can she teach the great
criteria and inalienable values, guide consciences
and offer a life choice that goes beyond the political sphere. To form consciences, to be the advocate
of justice and truth, to educate in individual and
political virtues: that is the fundamental vocation
of the Church in this area. And lay Catholics must
be aware of their responsibilities in public life;
they must be present in the formation of the necessary [public] consensus and in opposition to injustice.[14]

The church claims no right to dominate the secular
realm. But she has *every* right—in fact an obligation—to
engage secular authority and to challenge those wielding
it to live the demands of justice. In this sense, the
Catholic Church cannot stay, has never stayed, and *never
will* stay "out of politics." Politics involves the exercise of
power. The use of power has moral content and human

consequences. And the well-being and destiny of the human person is very much the concern, and the special competence, of the Christian community. It's no use arguing that we live in a "post-Christian" age. There is no such thing. God became man in the person of Jesus Christ. He died for our redemption. Then he rose again. The changes this brought to humanity and history are permanent and irreversible. Therefore, for those of us who describe ourselves as Catholic, we can be disciples and missionaries, or we can be apostates; but there's no room for anything else.

Freedom, Charles Péguy once wrote, is a system based on courage. Unfortunately, courage can be inconvenient. Our old friend Aristippus, the Greek philosopher, once told his colleague Diogenes, "If you would learn to be subservient to the king, you would not have to live on such garbage as beans." Diogenes answered, "If you had learned to live on beans, you would not have to flatter the king."

So finally we come again to the question: What belongs to Caesar, and what belongs to God? To Caesar we owe respect and prayers for our leaders (1 Timothy 2:2); respect for the law; obedience to proper authority; and service to the common good. It's a rather modest list. And note that *respect* is not subservience, or silence, or inaction, or excuse making, or acquiescence to grave evil in the public life we all share. In fact, ultimately, everything important about human life belongs not to God: our intellect, our talents, our free will; those we love; the beauty and goodness in the world; our souls, our moral integrity, our hope for eternal life. *These* are the things that matter. These are the things worth struggling to ennoble and defend. And none of them came from Tiberius or anyone who succeeded him.

We do owe Caesar one final thing: our witness not simply as loyal citizens but also as *faithful* ones. Henri Bergson once said that the motive power of democracy is love. For many years I didn't understand what he meant. So much of democratic life is filled with conflict, hyperbole, theatrics, and bad taste. But I think I know now. We serve our democratic institutions best when we *love* our country; when we nourish its greatest ideals through our own courage, honesty, and active political engagement. American Catholics may have carved out a "quasi-religious sweet spot," but its real name is complacency, and if it's true, we're betraying the best gifts we can offer our country: our Catholic identity and witness, and our love.

If we really love this country, and if we really treasure our faith, living our Catholic beliefs without excuses or apologies, and advancing them in the public square, are the best expressions of patriotism we can give to the nation. American Catholics need to be *more* Catholic, not less; and not simply "more Catholic," but more *authenti-*

cally and unselfishly Catholic—in the way we live our personal lives, and in our public words and actions. That includes our political choices.

We are citizens of heaven first. But just as God so loved the world that he sent his only Son, so the glory and the irony of the Christian life is this: The more truly we love God, the more truly we serve the world.

12.

AFTERWORD: SOME FINAL THOUGHTS

THERE'S AN ODD QUALITY to writing a book like this one. The author gets to watch American politics change, chameleon-like, right before his eyes. In the 2004 election, secular-leaning blues took a drubbing from religion-friendly reds. Much of the media had a panic attack. Columnists warned darkly of a new civil war; a coup by Christian fanatics; the baptizing of America into "Jesusland."[1]

But candidates are no dopes. They see what works. By late 2007, quite a few people running for office were talking about the value of faith to their public service. Republican Rudy Giuliani wooed evangelicals, despite his "pro-choice" abortion views. Reverend Leah Daughtry, a Pentecostal minister, was named chief executive for the 2008 Democratic convention. And the *New York Times*, covering a discussion sponsored by *Sojourners* magazine and broadcast by CNN, reported on the "journeys of faith" so vital to Hillary Clinton, Barack Obama, and John Edwards.[2]

These actions made good political sense. Data show that most Americans want their presidential candidate to be a religious person. It's also very likely that many candidates sincerely hold their religious beliefs. But the proof of a person's faith is *whether, how, and how much* it shapes his or her behavior, public leadership included. That's especially true when doing the right thing gets politically expensive.

Maybe we'll see a new Great Awakening. Maybe there's been a sea change in the piety of our political parties. Or maybe, as some skeptics have suggested, candidates have figured out that faith-talk can be a vaccine against religious critics, and the fashion will pass. It's always best to assume the honesty and goodwill of other people, including candidates for public office. It's also fair to look for the evidence of what people say they believe. As Scripture says, "You will know them by their fruits" (Matthew 7:20). That's the first and best voter guide ever written. And it's one the Internal Revenue Service has not (yet) taken issue with.

ONE OF THE ironies of the 2004 election was the number of non-Catholics, ex-Catholics, lax Catholics, and anti-Catholics who developed a sudden interest in who should receive Communion, and when.

Senator John Kerry, a Catholic Democrat, had differences with the church on abortion. His run for president triggered a national media frenzy over *if* and *where* Kerry might be denied Communion. "Wafer watch" stories dwarfed the serious moral issues behind Senator Kerry's problems with the church. They also distorted the meaning of Communion itself.

The Catholic Church is a web of relationships based on the most important relationship of all: Jesus Christ's gift of himself to us in the Eucharist for our salvation. None of us earns the gift of Christ's love. None of us "deserves" the Eucharist. The words of the centurion are just as true today as they were two thousand years ago: "Lord, I am not worthy to receive you, but only say the word and my [soul] will be healed" (Matthew 8:8).

As Catholics, we believe that the Eucharist is not just a symbol or a sacred meal or an important ritual expressing our community. Rather it is, quite literally, the body and blood of Jesus Christ. It's his living presence in our midst. This is what distinguishes the Catholic faith from nearly every Protestant community. In fact, it's one of the central Catholic beliefs that the Protestant Reformation eventually "protested."

The Eucharist remains today the source and summit of Catholic life. And like every Catholic generation before us, we need to take the following words of Saint Paul very seriously: "Whoever, therefore, eats the bread or drinks the cup of the Lord in an unworthy manner will

be guilty of profaning the body and blood of the Lord"
(1 Corinthians 11:27). We should also remember these
words of Saint Justin, the great martyr from the second
century: "No one may take part [in the Eucharist] unless
he believes that what we teach is true, has received baptism for the forgiveness of sins and new birth, and lives
in keeping with what Christ taught."

What's the lesson for Catholics? Fifty years ago, too
many of us avoided receiving Communion out of an excessive fear of our own sins. Today, far too many of us receive Communion unthinkingly, reflexively, with no
sense of the urgent need for our own self-examination,
humility, and conversion. Worse, too many Catholics receive the body and blood of Christ even when they ignore
or deny the teachings of his church.

When we sin by theft, lying, adultery, pride, gossip,
anger, envy, callousness to the poor, pornography, or indifference, we do not live "in keeping with what Christ
taught." We remove ourselves, by our actions, from friendship with God. That means we need to turn back to the
Sacrament of Penance before we receive Communion. In
fact, many of us today need a deeper devotion to confession
simply to regain a basic understanding of grace and sin.

Likewise, if we ignore or deny what the church
teaches, or refuse to follow what she teaches, we are not
"in communion" with the Catholic faith. We separate
ourselves from the community of believers. If we receive
Communion anyway, we engage in a lie.

Saying we're Catholic and then rejecting Catholic teaching is dishonest; it shows a lack of personal integrity. Even worse, if we then receive Communion, we violate the rights of every Catholic who *does* believe and *does* strive to live the faith fully and unselfishly. And that compounds a sin against honesty with a sin against justice and charity. Again, as Justin Martyr said, "No one may take part [in the Eucharist] unless he believes what we teach is true."

The recurrent debates over denying Catholic politicians Communion are usually marked by ignorance about the church and disregard for the real nature of the Eucharist. Denying anyone Communion is a grave matter. It can never be ruled out as a course of action, but it should be reserved for serious cases of public scandal where it can actually make a difference.

The church *always* expects Catholics who are living in grave sin or who deny the teachings of the church—whether they're highly visible officials or anonymous parishioners—to have the integrity to respect both the Eucharist and the faithful, and to refrain from receiving Communion. But especially because of their high public profile and the public confusion caused by their views, Catholic officials who act against Catholic teaching in their political service on a foundational matter like abortion should not present themselves for Communion.

But what if public officials do anyway? In their 2004 *Catholics in Political Life* statement, the U.S. bishops said:

Given the wide range of circumstances involved in arriving at a prudential judgment on a matter of this seriousness, we recognize that such decisions [to deny Communion to Catholics in political life] rest with the individual bishop in accord with the established canonical and pastoral principles. Bishops can legitimately make different judgments on the most prudent course of pastoral action. Nevertheless, we all share an unequivocal commitment to protect human life and dignity and to preach the Gospel in difficult times.[3]

Some bishops feel that America's national political life makes it unwise for any local bishop to act alone in matters like denying public officials Communion. But there are two problems with such an approach.

First, no uniformity exists in handling these matters in the United States nor anywhere in the world, nor has it been *required* by the Holy See beyond what already exists in Canon Law. Second, a national policy could make it impossible for any local bishop to act in a timely way; it would also intrude on a bishop's legitimate discretion in shepherding his own local church. Obviously, consultation with brother bishops is always a prudent course. Ultimately, though, in my own view, specific decisions to deny anyone Communion need to remain with the local bishop, not a national bishops' conference.

Of course, this opens those same local bishops to

pressure from Catholic groups who think that publicly humiliating political leaders resolves problems. Sometimes it may. But in a media environment where almost any kind of church admonition of a public figure is misportrayed as religious vigilantism, it can just as easily harden officials in their views. If Catholic political life is dominated by bickering over who will or will not be denied Communion, the real issue will be overlooked. The real issue is this: Many of the same American Catholics who are successful, assertive, and professionally well educated in their secular lives really know very little about the church, their faith, and what being "Catholic" requires. As long as that continues, we'll have petulant claims of conscience and equally petulant demands for punishment.

At this point, rather than evade three obvious questions, let me raise them myself. Here's the first. As a bishop, *what would I do* if a Catholic public official— a person publicly acting against Catholic teaching on a grave moral issue like abortion, euthanasia, human cloning, or embryonic stem cell research—presented himself for Communion? If the official is not from my local church (that is, the diocese I serve as bishop), and I receive no contrary guidance from his own bishop, I would not refuse him Communion. I would assume his honesty and goodwill. And I would advise my brother priests in the diocese to do the same.

But what if he *does* belong to my diocese? As a

bishop, I have a duty in charity to help Catholic officials understand and support church teaching on vital issues. That's never a matter for public theater; it's always a matter of direct, private discussion. If that failed, I would ask the official to refrain from receiving Communion. If he still presented himself, I would publicly ask him to not take Communion, and publicly explain why to my people and brother priests. If he *still* persisted, then, and only then, I would withhold Communion from him—because of his deliberate disregard of the rights of other Catholics and the unity of the church.

It's important to understand that denying anyone Communion is not primarily a "penalty" for the individual, and framing it that way misrepresents the meaning of the action. When the church withholds Communion from any person, she does so to protect the integrity of the Sacrament, defend the faith of her people, and call the individual to conversion. It's also important to remember that priests are not the "employees" of their bishop; they are his brothers in the Sacrament of Orders. Since it's usually local pastors—not the bishop—who face this difficult issue directly in the Communion line, they need the same room for reasonable pastoral discretion that a local bishop must have.

Obviously, there is one clear exception to this process. Catholics who actively and prominently work to advance permissive abortion or any other serious violation of human dignity, persons who *deliberately* treat the church, her people, and her sacraments as political theater to attack Catholic convictions and faith, should never present themselves for Communion and should never be surprised at being denied if they do.

Here's the second question. My friends often ask me if Catholics in genuinely good conscience can vote for "pro-choice" candidates. The answer is: *I* couldn't. Supporting a "right" to choose abortion simply masks and evades what abortion really is: the deliberate killing of innocent life. I know of nothing that can morally offset that kind of evil.

But I do know sincere Catholics who reason differently, who are deeply troubled by war and other serious injustices in our country, and they act in good conscience. I respect them. I don't agree with their calculus. What distinguishes such voters, though, is that they put real effort into struggling with the abortion issue. They don't reflexively vote for the candidate of "their" party. They don't accept abortion as a closed matter. They refuse to stop pushing to change the direction of their party on the abortion issue. They won't be quiet. They keep fighting for a more humane party platform—one that would vow to protect the unborn child. Their decision to vote for a "pro-choice" candidate is genuinely painful and never easy for them.

One of the pillars of Catholic thought is this: *Don't deliberately kill the innocent, and don't collude in allowing it.* We sin if we support candidates *because* they support a false "right" to abortion. We sin if we support "pro-choice" candidates without a truly proportionate reason for doing so—that is, a reason grave enough to outweigh our obligation to end the killing of the unborn. And what would such a "proportionate" reason look like? It would be a reason we could, with an honest heart, expect the unborn victims of abortion to accept when we meet them and need to explain our actions—as we someday will.

Finally, here's the third question. What if Catholics face an election where both major candidates are "pro-choice"? What should they do then? Here's the answer: They should remember that the "perfect" can easily become the enemy of the "good."

The fact that no ideal or even normally acceptable candidate exists in an election does not absolve us from taking part in it. As Catholic citizens, we need to work for the greatest good. The purpose of cultivating a life of prayer, a relationship with Jesus Christ, and a love for the church is to grow as a Christian disciple—to become the kind of Catholic adult who can properly exercise conscience and good sense in exactly such circumstances. There isn't one "right" answer here. Committed Catholics can make very different but equally valid choices: to vote for the major candidate who most closely fits the moral ideal, to vote for an acceptable third-party candidate who is unlikely to win, or to not vote at all. All of these choices can be legitimate. This is a matter for personal decision, not church policy.

The point we must never forget is this: We need to keep fighting for the sanctity of the human person, starting with the unborn child and extending throughout life. We abandon our vocation as Catholics if we give up; if we either drop out of political issues altogether or knuckle under to America's growing callousness toward human dignity.

We need to keep fighting. Otherwise we become what the Word of God has such disgust for: salt that has lost its flavor.

WILLIAM FAULKNER ONCE wrote that the past is never dead; it's not even really "past" because it teaches us in the present and guides us toward the future. I remembered those thoughts from Faulkner when a journalist friend of mine sent me the following note as I finished these pages. He wrote:

> American Catholics make up about 6 percent of a much larger global family of faith. I sometimes think that American parochialism is the original sin of Catholics in this country. Virtually every book on Catholic affairs, left, right, or center, reads as if American Catholicism were a self-contained

enterprise—maybe with a problematic relationship with Rome, but no real connection to anything, anyone or anywhere else. It's one of the reasons, I suspect, that American Catholics instinctively interpret any decision from Rome they don't like as an act of oppression. It never occurs to them that Rome might be thinking about the needs of the whole Church, the Church someplace else.

The world would be very different today if Catholics had "stayed out of politics" in Poland under the Communists, or the Philippines under Marcos, or Malawi under Banda. Would we really be better off if those regimes had endured because Catholics decided that good manners prevented them from speaking up? Obviously the United States is very different from authoritarian police states, but the point is this: At its best, the Catholic faith is a vital milieu in which expressions of civil society premised on human dignity and the common good can take shape. That's not theory. It's the lived experience of the 20th and early 21st centuries.

Overwhelmingly, Catholic opinion in other parts of the world, especially in the global South where two-thirds of the Catholic population today lives, favors traditional Catholic moral positions on issues such as abortion and marriage. So the

American situation is not a recalcitrant Catholic hierarchy versus the *sensus fidelium*—rather, it's the global *sensus fidelium* versus a narrow band of progressive opinion in the North.[4]

It's a fitting place to end a book like this. How we live as American Catholics matters beyond our borders—but not because we're smarter, or better, or more prophetic, or more theologically astute, or more technologically advanced, or wealthier than the church in the rest of the world. It matters because we're citizens of a country that exercises more power, in more ways, in more places than any other nation in history. And that has implications.

America's great witness to the world has always been its legacy of freedom. Despite its sins and flaws, our nation's history is finally a story of opportunity, religious harmony, respect for the human person, constitutional democracy, and the rule of law. These great achievements made America a beacon. Generations of Catholics have rightly embraced America as their own. But if our nation now exports other values—violence, greed, vulgarity, abortion, a rejection of children—American Catholics must work to change that or be held coresponsible.

We make the future of our country and our world by the history we create in our actions *now*. We need to remember why we're here.

ACKNOWLEDGMENTS

A new book always sounds like a good idea at the time. After all, "it will practically write itself." Later, during the author's long trek across the desert of aggravation and regret, it becomes hard to remember what the good part of the idea was. But in the end, if some readers find value in these pages, it was worth it, and many people deserve to be thanked.

I'm grateful to Chris Rose for suggesting this project and helping with the content throughout. I also want to thank George Weigel for pointing me toward Doubleday, and the Doubleday editors Bill Barry and Trace Murphy for supporting this project with their suggestions, patience, and talent.

I'm also grateful to Ryan Anderson, Lynne Gerken, Jennifer Kraska, Robert Royal, Mary Angelita Ruiz, David Scott, and Loredana Vuoto for their great help in elaborating the ideas in this book. It would not exist without them.

Thanks are due also to John Allen, Helen Alvaré, Gerard V. Bradley, Jeanette De Melo, Greg Erlandson, Robert P. George, James Hitchcock, Sean Innerst, Monsignor Richard Malone, and Jonathan Reyes, who all read portions of the text at various stages and offered kind and valuable criticism. Obviously, inadequacies in the text are mine alone. I'm grateful to Alejandro Bermúdez and Tracy Kmetz as well, who provided important help with the research. I also want to acknowledge in a special way Gail Quinn, whose work for the sanctity of human life over many years is a model of lay Catholic witness.

Finally, this book could never have been pursued and completed without the dedication and creative energy of my personal staff—in particular, Kerry Kober and Francis X. Maier. On this project, as with so many others, the value of their help cannot be quantified.

NOTES

1. STARTING AT THE SOURCE

1. U.S. Catholic bishops, *Living the Gospel of Life: A Challenge to American Catholics* (Washington, D.C.: U.S. Conference of Catholic Bishops, 1998).
2. From a November 10, 1889, homily celebrating the centenary of the Archdiocese of Baltimore.
3. Jim Rutenberg, "Media Talk; AOL Sees a Different Side of Time Warner," *New York Times*, March 19, 2001.
4. Christopher Lasch, *The Revolt of the Elites and the Betrayal of Democracy* (New York: Norton, 1995), pp. 25–26, 20.
5. "Interview with James Purefoy," *Rome* television series podcast, Home Box Office, hbo.com/rome/downloads/, November 24, 2005. Purefoy, probably without knowing it, echoed similar remarks about the impact of Christianity made nearly thirty years earlier by the actress Siân Phillips. Phillips portrayed Livia, the wife of Augustus Caesar, in the 1976 BBC adaptation of the Robert Graves novel *I Claudius*.

2. MEN WITHOUT CHESTS

1. "French Cardinal Urges Catholics to Follow Christianity in Election," Catholic News Service, April 12, 2007.

2. World Values Survey estimate, 1995–2000, Center for Applied Research in the Apostolate, Georgetown University, Washington, D.C., cara.georgetown.edu.

3. "The EU's Baby Blues," BBC News, March 27, 2006, news.bbc.co.uk/2/hi/europe/4768644.stm.

4. See David Rieff, "The Battle over the Banlieues," *New York Times Sunday Magazine*, April 15, 2007, for immigrant issues on the eve of the 2007 French election.

5. "Muslims in Europe: Integration Policies in Selected Countries," CRS Report for Congress, Paul Gallis, coordinator, with Kristin Archick, Francis Miko, and Steven Woehrel, Foreign Affairs, Defense, and Trade Division, Congressional Research Service, Library of Congress, November 18, 2005, pp. 3, 22. Other sources place the French Muslim population at approximately 5 million, and Europe's overall Muslim population between 12.5 and 15 million.

6. Joseph Ratzinger, St. Benedict Award Lecture, Subiaco, Italy, April 1, 2005.

7. Negative birthrate is now a problem for most developed countries, with serious social and economic implications. But it is especially pronounced in Europe. See, among many others, Niall Ferguson, "The Way We Live Now: 4–4–04; Eurabia?" *New York Times*, April 4, 2004.

8. Life expectancy statistics vary according to the standards of reporting organizations. Overall, the average U.S. life expectancy is somewhat lower than in western European countries, but higher than in China, Latin America, south and central Asia, and Africa.

9. Jay P. Greene, Ph.D., and James A. Winters, "Public High School Graduation and College-Readiness Rates, 1991–2002," Manhattan Institute for Policy Research, Education Working Paper no. 8, February 2005.

10. "Education Gap," Worldfund education data, worldfund.org.

11. "Secondary Education in Africa," World Bank education data, web.worldbank.org/.

12. Bureau of Economic Analysis, U.S. Department of Commerce data.

13. Robert J. Samuelson, *The Good Life and Its Discontents: The American Dream in the Age of Entitlement, 1945–1995* (New York: Times Books, Random House, 1995), p. 3.

14. Mental Health America (mentalhealthamerica.net/go/information/get-info/depression/depression-in-the-work place), citing P. E. Greenberg, L.E. Stiglin, S. N. Finkelstein, E. R. Berndt, "The Economic Burden of Depression in 1990," *Journal of Clinical Psychiatry* 2 (1993): 32–35.

15. Sung E. Son, M.D., and Jeffrey T. Kirchner, D.O., "Depression in Children and Adolescents," *American Family Physician*, American Academy of Family Physicians, November 15, 2000.

16. "Spendthrift Nation," Federal Reserve Bank of San Francisco Economic Letter 2005–30, November 10, 2005.

17. Sam Morris, "To Be Married Means to Be Outnumbered," reporting U.S. Census Bureau American Community Survey data, *New York Times,* October 15, 2006.

18. A survey by the Intercollegiate Studies Institute, *The Coming Crisis in Citizenship* (Wilmington, Del.: ISI, 2006), suggested that not only do students fail to learn more about vital American traditions at most elite U.S. universities; in many places, they actually forget material they were taught in high school.

19. The historian David McCullough, in testimony to the Senate Committee on Health, Education, Labor and Pensions, April 2003.

20. National Center for Education Statistics, Institute for Education Sciences, U.S. Department of Education, 2001, nces.ed.gov/nationsreportcard/ushistory/results/natachieve-g12.asp.

21. Bijal P. Trivedi, "Survey Reveals Geographic Illiteracy," National Geographic News, news.nationalgeographic.com/, November 20, 2002.

22. 2006 National Geographic–Roper Survey of Geographic Literacy, http://geosurvey.nationalgeographic.com/roper2006/findings.html. Note that various other developed countries have similar patterns of young adult indifference or ignorance, but none has the global responsibilities and influence of the United States.

23. Neil Postman, "My Graduation Speech," in *Conscientious Objections: Stirring Up Trouble About Language, Technology and Education* (New York: Vintage Books, 1992), pp. 185–90.

24. Samuelson, *The Good Life,* p. 4.

25. James B. Twitchell, *For Shame: The Loss of a Sense of Common Decency in American Culture* (New York: St. Martin's Press, 1997).

26. William Damon, *Greater Expectations: Overcoming the Culture of Indulgence in Our Homes and Schools* (New York: Free Press, 1996).

27. Charles Derber, *The Wilding of America: How Greed and Violence Are Eroding Our Nation's Character* (New York: St. Martin's Press, 1996), p. viii.

28. Jedediah Purdy, "Age of Irony," *American Prospect*, November 30, 2002.

29. International Institute for Democracy and Electoral Assistance data, idea.int/vt/survey/voter_turnout_pop2.cfm.

30. Jeffrey H. Birnbaum, "The Road to Riches Is Called K Street," *Washington Post*, June 22, 2005.

31. For a comprehensive look at today's revisionist critique of Christianity, including the rewriting of Christianity's role in Western history, see Vincent Carroll and David Shiflett, *Christianity on Trial: Arguments Against Anti-Religious Bigotry* (San Francisco: Encounter Books, 2002).

32. See Francis Collins, "Why This Scientist Believes in God," CNN News, April 6, 2007, cnn.com/; and Cornelia Dean, "Scientists Speak Up on Mix of God and Science," *New York Times*, August 23, 2005.

33. Richard Dawkins, "Religion's Misguided Missiles," *Guardian*, September 15, 2001; and "Is Science a Religion?" *Humanist* 57, no. 1 (January/February 1997).

34. "John Polkinghorne Q & A," starcourse.org/jcp/qanda.html.

35. See the Pew Forum on Religion and Public Life, "Religion and World Affairs," pewforum.org/world-affairs/.

36. Berger, director of the Institute on Culture, Religion and World Affairs at Boston University, took part in a Pew Research Center roundtable, "Secular Europe and Religious America: Implications for Transatlantic Relations," on April 21, 2005. At the time, he noted: "As long as you move in what I've called the 'faculty club culture' in the U.S., you may as well be in Europe. And that is very different from most of the population, and I think many of the political problems in the United States over the last 40 years or so have been a result of a strongly religious population rebelling against the secularity of an intelligentsia which is relatively small in numbers but very influential in the society."

37. Sam Harris, "Beyond the Believers," Council for Secular Humanism, secularhumanism.org.

38. C. S. Lewis, *The Abolition of Man* (New York: Macmillan, 1972).

39. B. F. Skinner, *Beyond Freedom and Dignity* (New York: Knopf, 1971), pp. 200–201.

40. Reinhold Niebuhr, *Christianity and Power Politics* (New York: Charles Scribner's Sons, 1940; reprint: Archon Books, 1969), p. 118.

41. Paul Johnson, "The Almost Chosen People," *First Things* 164 (June/July 2006).

42. Christian Smith, ed., *The Secular Revolution: Power, Interests and Conflict in the Secularization of American Public Life* (Los Angeles: University of California Press, 2003).

43. Baylor Religion Survey data.

44. Nancy Frazier-O'Brien, "Faith of Candidates, Voters May Have Role in Election, Surveys Find," Catholic News Service, June 22, 2007, reporting Sacred Heart Polling Institute and Gallup Poll News Service data.

45. 2006 Barna Update, the Barna Group, barna.org.

46. Neil Postman, *Amusing Ourselves to Death: Public Discourse in the Age of Show Business* (New York: Penguin Books, 1986), p. 112.

47. Christopher Dawson, *The Judgment of the Nations* (New York: Sheed and Ward, 1942), p. 99.

3. WHY WE'RE HERE

1. Viktor E. Frankl, *Man's Search for Meaning*, preface to the 1992 edition (Boston: Beacon Press, 2006), p. xiii.

2. Ibid., p. 37.

3. Pope John Paul II, *Familiaris Consortio*, Apostolic Exhortation on the Family, November 22, 1981, no. 11.

4. Pope Benedict XVI, *Deus Caritas Est*, Encyclical Letter on Christian Love, December 25, 2005, no. 28a.

5. Joseph Pearce, "J. R. R. Tolkien: Man and Myth," *Lay Witness* 22, no. 7 (September 2001).

6. Humphrey Carpenter, ed., with the assistance of Christopher Tolkien, *The Letters of J. R. R. Tolkien* (New York: Houghton Mifflin, 2000), p. 172.

7. Dietrich Bonhoeffer, *Dietrich Bonhoeffer: Writings Selected with an Introduction by Robert Coles* (Maryknoll, N.Y.: Orbis Books, 1998), p. 123.

8. Raissa Maritain, ed., *Léon Bloy: Pilgrim of the Absolute* (New York: Pantheon Books, 1947), p. 349.

9. Pope John Paul II, *Salvifici Doloris*, Apostolic Letter on the Christian Meaning of Human Suffering, February 11, 1984, no. 6.

10. Christopher Dawson, *Medieval Essays* (New York: Sheed and Ward), 1954, p. 57.

11. Bonhoeffer, *Ethics*, ed. Eberhard Bethge (New York: Macmillan, 1965), p. 104.

12. Pope Pius XI, *Mit Brennender Sorge*, Encyclical Letter on the Church and the German Reich, March 14, 1937, no. 19.

13. Ibid., no. 30.

14. Ibid., no. 33.

15. Niebuhr, *Christianity and Power Politics*, p. 217.

16. Carpenter, *Letters of J. R. R. Tolkien*, p. 116.

17. C. S. Lewis, "Christianity and Culture," from *The Seeing Eye and Other Selected Essays from Christian Reflections*, ed. Walter Hooper (New York: Ballantine Books, 1986), p. 44.

4. CONSTANTINE'S CHILDREN

1. "Courage in the Church," *New York Times*, April 19, 1962.

2. See Christopher Lasch, *The True and Only Heaven: Progress and Its Critics* (New York: Norton, 1991), pp. 14, 82–83, and especially 117–19 for a discussion of the gap between nostalgia and real memory, and the implications that follow. See also Lasch, *The Culture of Narcissism: American Life in an Age of Diminishing Expectations* (New York: Norton, 1979),

pp. xvii–xviii, 5–10, on "losing the sense of historical continuity."

3. See Romano Guardini, *The Death of Socrates: An Interpretation of the Platonic Dialogues: Euthyphro, Apology, Crito and Phaedo*, trans. from the German by Basil Wrighton (New York: Meridian Books, 1962), as a guide to this dynamic.

4. Origen, *Contra Celsum*, 75, c. 230.

5. Ibid., 73.

6. Hippolytus, *Apostolic Tradition*, 16:9–11, c. 215.

7. Tatian, *Address to the Greeks*, 11, c. 160.

8. Maurice, *Maurice's Strategikon: Handbook of Byzantine Military Strategy*, trans. George T. Dennis (Philadelphia: University of Pennsylvania Press, 1984), p. 8.

9. Unsigned, "A Kingdom of Martyrs: The Politics of Christendom," agnology.com, May 21, 2007.

10. Jean-Jacques Rousseau, *The Social Contract*, trans. with an introduction by Wilmoore Kendall (Chicago: Regnery Gateway, 1954), p. 209.

11. Pope Gelasius I, Letter to Emperor Anastasius on Spiritual and Temporal Power, trans. in J. H. Robinson, *Readings in European History* (Boston: Ginn, 1905), pp. 72–73.

12. Thomas Aquinas, *Summa Theologiae*, Ia IIa, 100.2.

13. See Robert P. Kraynak, *Christian Faith and Modern Democracy: God and Politics in the Fallen World* (Notre Dame, Ind.: University of Notre Dame Press, 1996).

14. Paul Johnson, *A History of Christianity* (New York: Atheneum, 1977), p. 75.

15. Rodney Stark, *The Rise of Christianity: How the Marginal Jesus Movement Became the Dominant Religious Force in the Western*

World in a Few Centuries (San Francisco: HarperSanFrancisco, 1997), p. 211.

16. Ibid., p. 208.

17. Ibid., p. 211.

18. Dawson, *The Judgment of the Nations*, pp. 186–87.

19. Lasch, *The Revolt of the Elites*, p. 221.

20. Ibid., p. 243.

5. THE AMERICAN EXPERIMENT

1. Kate Mason Rowland, *The Life of Charles Carroll of Carrollton, 1737–1832* (New York: G. P. Putnam's Sons, 1898), p. 181.

2. See acton.org/publications/randl/rl_liberal_en_368.php, February 16, 2007. For further reading on Charles Carroll, see Milton Lomask, *Charles Carroll and the American Revolution* (New York: P. J. Kenedy and Sons, 1959); and Thomas O'Brien Hanley, *Charles Carroll of Carrollton: The Making of a Revolutionary Gentleman* (Chicago: Loyola Press, 1982).

3. Chester Gillis, *Roman Catholicism in America* (New York: Columbia University Press, 1999), pp. 52–56.

4. Daniel J. Boorstin, *The Americans: The Colonial Experience* (New York: Random House, 1958), pp. 132–39, 308.

5. See Alexander Hamilton, James Madison, and John Jay, *The Federalist Papers* (Norwalk, Conn.: Easton Press, 1979), originally published 1787–88. See also Jackson Turner Main, *The Antifederalists, Critics of the Constitution, 1781–1788* (New York: Norton, 1961).

6. See churchstatelaw.com/historicalmaterials/8_2_5.asp. See also Alexis de Tocqueville, *Democracy in America*, part 1 (New York: Everyman's Library, 1972), pp. 300–314.

7. Pope Leo XIII, *Longinqua Oceani*, Encyclical Letter on Catholicism in the United States, January 6, 1895, no. 6.

8. See especially Murray's essays "Leo XIII on Church and State: The General Structure of the Controversy," *Theological Studies,* March 1953; and "Leo XIII: Separation of Church and State," *Theological Studies*, June 1953, both available from woodstock.georgetown.edu/library/Murray/0_murraybib .html.

9. John Courtney Murray, S.J., *We Hold These Truths: Catholic Reflections on the American Proposition* (New York: Sheed and Ward, 1960), p. ix.

6. A NEW DISPENSATION

1. Pope Saint Gregory VII, recounted in Dawson, *Medieval Essays,* p. 72.

2. John Henry Newman, "The Ventures of Faith," in *Parochial and Plain Sermons,* vol. 4, no. 20 (San Francisco: Ignatius Press, 1997), p. 926.

3. Joseph Ratzinger, *Theological Highlights of Vatican II* (New York: Paulist Press, 1966), pp. 95–96.

4. Ibid., pp. 22–23; but see also pp. 11 and 20–21 for frank descriptions of preconciliar mentalities and the early issues faced by the council.

5. Neil Postman, *Technopoly: The Surrender of Culture to Technology* (New York: Vintage Books, 1993), p. 20.

6. Avery Dulles, S.J., *The Resilient Church: The Necessity and Limits of Adaptation* (New York: Doubleday, 1977), p. 64.

7. Pope John XXIII, *Mater et Magistra*, Encyclical Letter on Christianity and Social Progress, May 15, 1961, no. 1.

8. Pope John XXIII, *Gaudet Mater Ecclesia*, Opening Address to the Second Vatican Council, October 11, 1962.

9. Yves Congar, O.P., *Vraie et Fausse Réforme dans l'Église* (Paris: Cerf, 1950), p. 339, as referenced by Marcellino D'Ambrosio. See D'Ambrosio's *"Ressourcement* Theology, *Aggiornamento* and the Hermeneutics of Tradition," *Communio International Theological Review* 18 (Winter 1991), for an excellent overview of *ressourcement* theology's impact at the council.

10. Henri de Lubac, S.J., *The Drama of Atheist Humanism*, trans. Edith M. Riley (New York: Meridian Books, 1963), p. 72.

11. *Decree on Ecumenism*, no. 6.

12. Dulles, *The Resilient Church*, p. 1.

13. Ratzinger, *Theological Highlights of Vatican II*, p. 5.

14. Ibid., pp. 7–8.

15. Quotations from all conciliar documents are drawn from Austin Flannery, O.P., general editor, *Vatican Council II: The Conciliar and Post-Conciliar Documents*, vol. 1, new revised edition (Grand Rapids, Mich.:, William Eerdmans, 1992).

16. Ratzinger, *Theological Highlights of Vatican II*, pp. 184–85.

7. WHAT WENT WRONG

1. Joseph Ratzinger, "The Future of the World Through the Hope of Men," in *Faith and the Future* (Chicago: Franciscan Herald Press, 1971), pp. 80, 85; originally presented on Vatican Radio in February 1970.

2. Joseph Ratzinger, "Why I Am Still in the Church," in *Two Say Why* (Chicago: Franciscan Herald Press, 1973), p. 67.

3. Ibid., p. 86; see also his thoughts on the work of Freud, Jung, Marcuse, et al., p. 85.

4. See Ratzinger, *Two Say Why*, p. 71, on the motives of some who applauded the council.

5. See John Lamont, "What Was Wrong with Vatican II," *New Blackfriars* 88, no. 1013 (January 2007).

6. See Lasch, *The True and Only Heaven: Progress and Its Critics*, pp. 21–24.

7. Joseph Ratzinger with Vittorio Messori, *The Ratzinger Report: An Exclusive Interview on the State of the Church* (San Francisco: Ignatius Press, 1985), p. 24.

8. "Forgetting Religion," *Washington Post*, March 22, 1931.

9. Pope Benedict XVI, *Sacramentum Caritatis*, Apostolic Exhortation on the Eucharist as the Source and Summit of the Church's Life and Mission, February 22, 2007.

10. Ratzinger, *The Ratzinger Report*, p. 19.

11. See *Nostra Aetate*, 2, 4. See also *Dominus Iesus,* Declaration on the Unicity and Salvific Universality of Jesus Christ and the Church, Congregation for the Doctrine of the Faith, August 6, 2000.

12. Ratzinger, *Les Principes de la Theologie Catholique: Esquisse et Materiaux* (Paris: Tequi, 1982), pp. 426–27; passage translated by Robert Royal. The work's full-text English translation appears as *Principles of Catholic Theology: Building Stones for a Fundamental Theology* (San Francisco: Ignatius Press, 1987); see pp. 381–82.

13. Mary Eberstadt, *"Gaudium et Spes,"* in *A Century of Catholic Social Thought: Essays on Rerum Novarum and Nine Other Key Documents*, ed. George Weigel and Robert Royal (Washington, D.C.: Ethics and Public Policy Center, 1990), p. 89.

14. For an analysis of the environment facing Kennedy, as well as Kennedy's "theological vapidity" and "stark new vision of an exceedingly high and solid wall of separation between church and state," see Mark S. Massa, S.J., "A Catholic for President? John F. Kennedy and the 'Secular' Theology of the Houston Speech, 1960," Baylor University, J. M. Dawson Institute for Church-State Studies, *Journal of Church and State*, March 1997. As Massa notes, the Houston speech involved an "almost-total privatization of [Kennedy's] Catholic faith." In fact, "the secularity that the speech [advocated] represented a near-total privatization of religious belief—so much a privatization that religious observers from both sides of the Catholic/Protestant fence commented on its remarkable atheistic implications for public life and discourse."

15. Kennedy's Houston comments quoted here are available in text and audio formats at jfklibrary.org.

16. William Lee Miller, *The First Liberty* (New York: Knopf, 1986), p. 286.

17. For Murray's "separationist" remark, see letter quoted in Mark S. Massa, S.J., *Catholics and American Culture: Fulton Sheen, Dorothy Day and the Notre Dame Football Team* (New York: Crossroad, 1999), pp. 143–44. Murray's reported "idiocy" comment is widely quoted but difficult to verify; in fact, it may actually derive from Murray's 1962 essay "The Return to Tribalism," where he argues, "What is our contemporary idiocy? What is the enemy within the city? If I had to give it a name, I think I would call it 'technological secularism.' The idiot today is the technological secularist who knows everything. He's the man who knows everything about the organization of all the instruments and techniques of power that are available in the contemporary world and who, at the same time, understands nothing about the nature of man or about the nature of true civilization." Murray's reported personal preference for Richard Nixon as the 1960 presidential candidate is equally hard to confirm. Nonetheless, given Murray's body of thought, it is unlikely that he would have endorsed the drastic kind of separationism advanced in Kennedy's Houston speech.

8. CONSCIENCE AND COWARDICE

1. Stephen Colbert, "The Word: Truthiness," *The Colbert Report*, October 17, 2005, comedycentral.com.

2. Nathan Rabin, "Interviews: Stephen Colbert," A. V. Club, January 25, 2006, avclub.com.

3. George Orwell, "Politics and the English Language," in *The*

Orwell Reader: Fiction, Essays and Reportage, with an introduction by Richard H. Rovere (New York: Harcourt, 1984), pp. 355–66.

4. Postman, *Amusing Ourselves to Death*, p. 43.

5. Ibid., p. 87.

6. Bill McKibben, *The Age of Missing Information* (New York: Plume/Penguin, 1993), p. 9.

7. Neil Postman, "The Parable of the Ring Around the Collar," in *Conscientious Objections*, p. 67.

8. John Henry Newman, "Letter to the Duke of Norfolk."

9. Newman, "Letter to Mrs. William Froude."

10. Newman, "Sermons Preached on Various Occasions," no. 5, "Dispositions for Faith."

11. George Weigel, *Catholicism and the Renewal of American Democracy* (New York: Paulist Press, 1989), pp. 89–90.

12. Murray, *We Hold These Truths*, p. 42.

13. Ibid., p. 21.

14. Ibid.

15. Ibid., p. 13.

16. Martin Luther King Jr., "Letter from Birmingham Jail," available from stanford.edu/group/King/frequentdocs/birmingham.pdf; for the "Statement of Alabama Clergymen" that sparked it, see stanford.edu/group/King/frequentdocs/clergy.pdf.

9. A MAN FOR ALL SEASONS

1. Quoted in James Monti, *The King's Good Servant but God's First: The Life and Writings of St. Thomas More* (San Francisco: Ignatius Press, 1997), p. 15; originally from G. K. Chesterton, "A Turning Point in History," 1929.
2. See Hilaire Belloc, *Wolsey* (Philadelphia: Lippincott, 1930). Belloc's portrait of the cardinal as a man defined by three attributes—high intelligence, lack of vision, and intense personal ambition—may not be completely fair, but it does capture the moral gulf between Wolsey and More.
3. See *Utopia*, prefatory letter to Peter Giles, *Collected Works*, 4:39–41.
4. See the 1519 letter in which Erasmus describes his friend Thomas More, stthomasmore.net/erasmus.html, taken from T. E. Bridgett, *Life and Writings of Blessed Thomas More* (London: Burns Oates, 1913).
5. Robert H. Bork, "Thomas More for Our Season." *First Things* 94 (June/July 1999).
6. Governor Mario Cuomo, "Religious Belief and Public Morality: A Catholic Governor's Perspective," remarks at the University of Notre Dame, September 13, 1984, pewforum.org/docs/index.php?DocID=14.
7. Governor Robert P. Casey, untitled address, Center for Ethics and Culture, University of Notre Dame, 1995, ethicscenter.nd.edu/archives/casey1995.shtml.
8. Ibid.

9. Ibid.

10. Robert P. Casey, *Fighting for Life* (Dallas: Word, 1996), p. 245, originally from a Casey commencement address, Franciscan University of Steubenville, May 14, 1994.

11. Gerard Wegemer, *Thomas More on Statesmanship* (Washington, D.C.: Catholic University of America Press, 1996), p. 210.

12. Ibid.

10. WHAT NEEDS TO BE DONE

1. Avery Dulles, S. J., "Catholicism and American Culture: The Uneasy Dialogue," *America*, January 27, 1990.

2. See Lasch, *The True and Only Heaven*, pp. 33–34. No better portrait of America's shadow side exists than the one penned by Lasch—never a man of the political Right—in describing the impact of becoming a parent on his views as a social and cultural critic. He wrote, "The unexpectedly rigorous business of bringing up children exposed me, as it necessarily exposes every parent, to our 'child-centered' society's icy indifference to everything that makes it possible for children to flourish and to grow up to be responsible adults. To see the modern world from the point of view of a parent is to see it in the worst possible light." Among the many signs of destructive "unwholesomeness" in modern American life, he noted "our inhospitable attitude to the newcomers born into our midst, our unstated assumption, which underlies so much of the propaganda for unlimited abortion, that only

those children born for success ought to be allowed to be born at all."

3. Russell Shaw, *Catholic Laity in the Mission of the Church* (Bethune, S.C.: Requiem Press, 2005), pp. 162–64.

4. See text in *Weapons of the Spirit: Selected Writings of Father John Hugo*, ed. David Scott and Mike Aquilina (Huntington, Ind.: Our Sunday Visitor, 1997), pp. 93–95.

5. One area where the church does urgently need to focus more resources, planning, and personnel, and where such things can make a difference, is her ministry to Latino immigrants and the wider Latino community. But even here, we should be wary about assuming that a larger U.S. Latino population will automatically refresh or sustain Catholic life. See Laurie Goodstein, "For Some Hispanics, Coming to America Also Means Abandoning Religion," *New York Times*, April 15, 2007. See also the Pew Hispanic Center study *Changing Faiths: Latinos and the Transformation of American Religion*, pewhispanic.org, April 25, 2007. About a third of all American Catholics now have Latino roots, but Latinos also now leave the Catholic Church for evangelical churches, or no church at all, in growing numbers. Statistically, the secularizing effect of U.S. political and consumer culture hits Latinos about as hard as every other ethnic group.

6. On the anti-Catholic motives behind much of modern church-state jurisprudence, see Daniel Dreisbach, *Thomas Jefferson and the Wall of Separation Between Church and State* (New York: New York University Press, 2003); Philip Hamburger, *Separation of Church and State* (Cambridge, Mass.: Harvard

University Press, 2004); John T. McGreevy, "Thinking on One's Own: Catholicism in the American Intellectual Imagination, 1928–1960," *Journal of American History* 84, no. 1 (June 1997): 97–131.

7. *Mitchell v. Helms,* 530 U.S. 793, 2000.

8. Archbishop F. X. Nguyen Van Thuan, *The Road of Hope: A Message from Captivity to My People* (New York: Wethersfield Institute, 1995), p. 169.

9. Saint Hilary of Poitiers, "Against Emperor Constantius," text in Hugo Rahner, *Church and State in Early Christianity* (San Francisco: Ignatius Press, 1992), p. 91.

10. The story of Saint Basil's confrontation with Emperor Valens is told in Rahner, *Church and State in Early Christianity*, p. 63.

11. Saint Hilary of Poitiers, "Against Emperor Constantius," text in Rahner, *Church and State in Early Christianity*, p. 90.

12. Pope John Paul II, *Redemptoris Missio,* Encyclical Letter on the Permanent Validity of the Church's Missionary Mandate, December 7, 1990, no. 11.

13. Pope Benedict XVI, *Deus Caritas Est*, Encyclical Letter on Christian Love, December 25, 2005, no. 18.

14. Pope John Paul II, *Centesimus Annus*, Encyclical Letter on the 100th Anniversary of *Rerum Novarum*, May 1, 1991, no. 54.

11. FAITHFUL CITIZENS

1. David Brooks, *Bobos in Paradise: The New Upper Middle Class and How They Got There* (New York: Simon and Schuster, 2000), pp. 10, 11, 14.